The Intimacy Manual

Balancing Control and Intimacy in the Bedroom and the Boardroom

Edmund J. Amidon

Marilyn G. Amidon

Jack A. Apsche

Michael L. Silverman

Eugene H. Stivers

International Information Associates, Inc.
Morrisville

Library of Congress Catalog No.: 91-75958
Amidon, Edmund J.
Amidon, Marilyn G.
Apsche, Jack A.
Silverman, Michael L.
Stivers, Eugene H.
***The Intimacy Manual*:**
Balancing Intimacy and Control in the Bedroom and the Boardroom

ISBN 0-945510-08-X

International Information Associates, Inc.
P.O. Box 773, Morrisville, PA 19067, U.S.A.

Current printing [last digit]:
10 9 8 7 6 5 4 3 2 1

Printed in the United States of America

Messages in Intimacy and Control, Loneliness and Conflict

From the beginning, this work takes the view that we all are individuals trying to find our way in relationships or groups. Issues of intimacy and control which are present when we start these relationships persist and seem to need answers at many points in the process. The basic questions we ask ourselves and the others involved are, "How close should we be?" and "Who will be in control?"

Sometimes we have difficulty with the questions because of assumptions we hold about intimacy and control. Most of us learn about intimacy and control from our early relationships in the family and at school. This early learning has continuous influence on how we perceive, react and develop within our later relationships and groups.

One such early learning for most people, which then becomes a continuing assumption, is that every member of a group needs to adjust to the others in order to remain a satisfied and productive group member. This very process of adjustment often seems to produce conflict, loneliness, or even division among members. But in some cases, members may observe that the adjustment-conflict-loneliness cycle goes on to facilitate the development of reconciliation, cooperation, and intimacy.

For most people, one of the clearest group issues is the development of ways to "work through" such periods of adjustment. The authors take the point of view that this adjustment is seen in terms of intimacy and control: How close do I want to be? How close should I get for most effective group functioning? How close for my own comfort? How can the intimacy level be mediated when members in a relationship want different levels of intimacy? These questions must be negotiated again and again in relationships.

The same kind of analysis can be applied to issues of control. How much freedom will I have in this group or relationship? If I join will I lose more control of my life than I can tolerate? How will control be distributed in the relationship? What will happen if I want equality in control and the other person wants to be in control or to be controlled?

It seems apparent that the issues of closeness and control are interrelated. That is, one may feel less (more) powerful as one becomes (more) less intimate. Upon approaching marriage, for example, many people say or think, "As our relationship becomes closer, I feel fearful that I may lose some control over my life." The process of increasing involvement in a group or relationship produces these questions for everyone at some level.

The approach presented here is that such interpersonal and group processes can be understood, and that these understandings (along with appropriate procedures and techniques) may help us make more intelligent choices as our relationships develop.

The Purpose of the Book

We will provide a procedure for investigating the aspects of intimacy and control in messages we send to and receive from one another as well as the internal messages we send to ourselves. The book will also develop an understanding of these two concepts as they apply to basic processes in relationships or small groups.

The concepts in the book represent those basic processes relevant to all types of groups and relationships. Yet because of their threatening nature, issues of intimacy and control are often avoided and as a result, we do not work at understanding them.

How can we expect to open up the topic of messages of intimacy and control in our lives? How can we look at these issues in our groups, relationships, and organizations? What is offered here that would provide insight into what might be thought of as difficult, perhaps even dangerous topics?

The answers found in the book are operational if not necessarily definitive or "foolproof."

Our approach here offers three basic tools for the the reader:

1. The book itself is a message. The message is a model, and the model is easy to adapt to any situation. It is a basic feedback model. That is, the user of the book is provided with ideas and structures

which are designed to help the reader go through simple procedures which produce feedback about specific behavior or attitudes.

2. The tools and techniques presented allow the reader to acquire valuable information about his/her attitudes, perceptions and behaviors.

3. Exercises and structured experiences are provided so that the reader may practice skills or behaviors (s)he is trying to develop.

This book provides an approach to the study of relationships and groups that can be used for analysis of any type of group or organization. For example,

In *the family,* control is an issue as parents struggle with each other and with the children.

In *the classroom,* we know that control has increasingly become an issue. Intimacy is also an issue, acknowledged or not.

In *the corporation,* effective control is often the difference between profit and loss—the so-called "bottom line."

The *salesperson,* who doesn't understand how or why the sale was lost, when it seemed that the relationship with the customer was a good one, may think (s)he somehow lost out on both intimacy and control.

In *relationships* with clients, the human services professional wants to understand more about her/his interactions with clients.

The *organizational worker* who believes that strategies are necessary for success wants to know more about control.

The *chairperson* of an important meeting, who accepts the importance of that meeting, is sometimes frustrated in repeated attempts to make it more efficient and productive.

The *husband* who notices that he and his wife "don't talk much any more" wonders what he can do about it.

The book provides approaches that may be used in virtually any interpersonal, group or organizational situation. A sequential model is provided for use: the reader may decide for him/herself what to do. The model leads the reader to develop ideas about how a relationship or group is changing over time. The leader, facilitator, therapist or group member can use this knowledge to determine appropriate actions. Neither predictions nor prescriptions are supplied—rather a *process* which can be implemented to produce desired change.

The approach here suggests ways that the reader can use his/her own resources to solve problems and enjoy satisfaction in the process.

The model provides a structure the reader can use to lead her/himself through the interpersonal issues which present themselves in group and organizational contacts.

The material in the book has been developed, tested and refined in graduate and undergraduate level classes in the Psychoeducational Processes program at Temple University beginning in 1976. The authors wish to point out that the book has been a group effort which involved students and colleagues at Temple University. Those graduate students who have been co-teachers in the courses which have been offered regularly since 1976, and those whose doctoral research has contributed to the development of the tools and techniques have been particularly helpful: Beverly Arsht, Charles Ashbach, Marsha Avery, Constance Bails, George Beck, Norma Bolden, Timothy Brigham, Sophie Bronstein, Edward Christian, Frances Clarida, Elaine Comer, Wallace Crider, Thomas Cullen, Patricia Darrah, Timothy Doris, Chiara Eash, Susan Edgar, Elise Freed-Fagan, Arline Getzoff-Goldstone, Elaine Getzow, Peggy Hullinger, Raphael Kavanaugh, Carla Kirsch, Patricia Kolosowski-Gager, Sylvia Kunreuther, Elisa Lang, Louise Merves-Okin, Thomas Platt, Paul Poplawski, Jeffrey Roth, Elinor Rozecki, Leslie Sandler, Sherrie Saner, Helma Silverstein, Pamela Stepanovich, Judith Strauss, William Tamblyn, Curt Torell, Thomas Treadwell, Jeanette Turner, Janet Widra and Nancy Youngblood.

And last but not least we wish to thank Ms. Alice B. Jackson who provided important help in the preparation of the manuscript.

Table of Contents

CHAPTER 7
Self-Intimacy and Self-Control

CHAPTER 1

Introduction

Wherever we are now in our lives, we can think of where we have been, where we are and where we are going as scenes in a journey from birth to death. Along the way we take part in relationships with others. We see...we meet...we talk...we experience...we compete...we fall in love...we separate. We move through many relationships. In all of it we are singular individuals with our own perceptions of ourselves and our performance, our perceptions of others and their performance, and even our own perceptions or guesses of their perceptions.

When we begin to relate to another person we wonder what the future will be. Will the relationship be related to control or to intimacy? Will I attempt to control, to share control or to give up control to this other person? Wanting intimacy or control in a relationship is not a static condition. In every relationship we move back and forth between intimacy and control in varying degrees. If a relationship is to grow and develop, not only is our choice of intimacy or control important, but also how we express our desires for intimacy and/or control.

We tend to pair intimacy and control. Could that be right... are they not at opposite poles? They seem far apart, and yet the conditions for striving for either one of them are so close as to be identical. What is the common thread that keeps intimacy and control so closely entwined? The desire for intimacy and the desire for control both test and stretch us intellectually, emotionally and physically. Passion is the connection, our zest for living, the life motivator, the catalyst. We humans will have these times of passion again and again in our lives. Our goal in this book is to create a structure for understanding our relationships with others. The ideas used to create the structure are intimacy and control.

In relating to others we have the potential to learn more and more about ourselves. We gain information about how we are perceived by others and how we behave toward others. We receive feedback on our actions toward or against others; we get involved and relieve our loneliness. We attract people and repel them, and in turn are attracted and repelled, but we shall relate and be passionate.

We are all creatures with personal frameworks, rituals, and systems. When we can arrange information to fit into our own personal understanding or framework we create comfort and feelings of control within ourselves. We are about to introduce frameworks that you may want to add to your personal maps and charts.

These frameworks interrelate as a three dimensional system for looking at our relationship behavior, taking into account the intellectual, the emotional and the physical/behavioral aspects of each of us.

Control is one of the two major concepts that will be used to consider our behavior. This concept is often thought about in terms of being at a "higher level." A person who feels (s)he has less control or power than another might complain that the other "looks down on me."

A Pedestal Theory of Communication

We have all heard of people who, when they feel intimidated or fall in love, tend to place the other person upon a pedestal. At the same time, when people are feeling superior or in greater control they may place themselves upon the pedestal looking down upon the other person. At still other times, the two individuals stand face to face and relate on equal terms. This may be thought of as a pedestal theory of communication. We tend to relate to each other based on our concept of ourselves in relation to another and our perceptions of the way that other relates to us.

If this scheme looks familiar, it's because it is based on and similar to Eric Berne's Transactional Analysis concepts of parent, adult and child. When I am feeling ONE-UP, I am feeling better (more powerful) than you, and in my eyes you are ONE-DOWN. My communication and behavior in relation to you will be affected by this inner judgment. If I am feeling ONE-DOWN, I am placing myself below you and will behave toward you as though I am less than you. If I am feeling that we are EVEN with each other I can relate to you directly and without manipulation. This seems simple, but keep in mind that one's own *perception* of the relationship at a given time is just that: an individual's perception. The object of my attention also has his/her perceptions with regard to him/herself and me. In relationships it is important to be aware of our own perceptions and also conscious of the perceptions of others.

Where I see myself in relation to the other person is the inner game that determines the outward behavior strategy that I will employ toward or away from the other person, and vice versa.

The other important concept used here is intimacy or closeness to another person or persons.

From the point of view of verbal communication, the least interactive contact is a conversation that appears outside the personal concerns of those people who are talking together. Often such a conversation is perfunctory or may be viewed as "small talk." Conversation that is more intimate is personal, of concern to those involved in a relationship, and includes feelings as well.

A Few Vignettes

Not a day too soon, but at least it saved John Morgan some trouble, trouble that he had been dreading. He had initially been attracted to Pat, an attractive woman trying to do a "man's job" in the big XYZ organization. She always seemed to like meeting with John. After a time though, John began to enjoy it less and less. He did enjoy the opportunity to watch her and perhaps have a little fantasy. He even asked her if she wanted to have their weekly "individual manager's conference" over coffee after work one Friday.

Pat showed great interest and added, "That's great! I like more informal meetings." John agreed, and he even let his fantasy soar. He had a specific agenda for this particular meeting. Pat's monthly performance report seemed to have some incomplete sections. Some of the statements she had made about her client contacts seemed to differ from the reports that potential customers had made. It didn't seem serious, but when several "good customers" reported no contact with their corporate representative, and Pat reported that she was making good contacts by phone and in person, John felt they had to talk.

The meeting at a local coffee shop was pleasant, and soon John forgot about "several good customers." Pat suggested that maybe they ought to just relax, that they could talk business later at her apartment. John relished this opportunity, but he was aware of a nagging fear.

They did go to her apartment and Pat was everything that John had hoped and feared. No business was discussed, but John was attracted beyond what he had thought possible.

Later, as he walked to his car he felt puzzled by his reluctance to get involved with Pat. He had kissed her (or maybe she had kissed him). It was the sort of kiss he liked, but it bothered him that she had managed not to explain the discrepancies in her report. It was these two facts, her kiss and her apparent lack of interest in business, that made him stand up and say "I really need to go home and prepare for our monthly sales meeting." As he left, Pat suggested that he come back the next night for dinner.

John didn't call Pat. He became more concerned when she missed the sales meeting, but was then relieved when he received a message the next day that she had been unable to attend because she had scheduled a meeting with one of those good customers who earlier reported that he had not heard from her.

John decided to follow up by calling the customer. He talked to Ralph Simms, the company manager. To describe Ralph's reaction as positive would be an understatement. He went on and on about his attitudes, ideas, and business instincts. John decided to listen, and the more he heard the more he wondered. It seemed that Ralph thought Pat should do some special jobs for him as part of her service to Ralph's company. John agreed that "when a representative makes a sale, then the representative should be available for service calls."

There hadn't actually been any orders placed, but the service work was necessary. In fact, Pat needed to spend several days working with Ralph. After this, John said he'd look into it and hung up the phone.

He then called XYZ Vice President Roger Kilgore and asked him what he thought of Ralph's idea. Roger didn't respond at once. After a period of noticeable silence he said, "We may have a problem. There have been complaints. You need to talk to her. What's she like, anyway?"

As John explained everything to Roger, the whole story unfolded. Roger had heard complaints about Pat, and he became as concerned as John.

The next day Roger called John to tell him that Pat had resigned and gone to work for Ralph. John was relieved, to say the least. He had been saved from having to confront Pat with what would have been painful facts. She had done no work with any of the customers. It appeared from what he now knew that she was using her resources as a stepping stone to a more attractive position.

This vignette raises questions for anyone who works in an organization. Although it brings to mind the caveat about mixing business with pleasure, our goal is to understand how situations like the one described can be managed successfully. The issues raised here and certainly related to intimacy, but clearly the focus is sexual attraction, manipulation and control. The concern of persons involved in relationships within an organization may be seen when the intimacy issue seems entwined, mixed or confused with the issue of control. What are the apparent symbols of intimacy? Is the goal to facilitate working together by becoming closer, or is attraction used to manipulate the other person?

Mary and Bill had a long and tumultuous dating relationship. Their children from previous marriages had adjusted, and actually seemed happy that the couple was finally getting married. There were problems, so the couple decided to see a marriage counselor.

Bill had first seen Mary in a neighborhood bar that seemed to cater to middle aged people. Bill liked to go to bars alone. He hoped to meet a beautiful woman who was instantly attracted to him. He had never been to this bar before; he suspected that its location in an exclusive condominium might attract the "wealthy and snobbish". Bill thought of himself as egalitarian and he would certainly not be interested in rich, exclusive or snobbish women (or men, for that matter).

As he entered the bar, Bill was pleased that two women came over and started talking to him. He thought, "This looks like a middle age male paradise." It seemed that most of the patrons were women who were 35-50 years in age. Bill discovered that many of them lived in the exclusive building or the surrounding area.

The women who approached Bill when he first entered were attractive, and seemed attracted to him. As Bill stood and talked, he noticed a woman seated at the end of the bar. She noticed him as well, and although she didn't smile he was aware that she was aware of him. Bill was also aware of his attractiveness to women. He knew that women seemed to like him, and his experience this night was an example of how they "came after him."

Although the two women who initially contacted him were attractive, Bill kept checking at the end of the bar to see if the blonde with glasses was still glancing at him. He saw that she was, and decided to meet her.

Bill feared that he "talked funny" when he tried to approach women to whom he felt attracted. Even so, he walked over to the bar, stood next to the blonde wearing glasses and ordered a non alcoholic beer. That got her attention. "That's funny, I had you pegged for a martini drinker." "Well, I am," said Bill, "but I didn't want to get bombed and fall down right next to you. You can tell that I am attracted to you."

Well, that's how it all started. Ten years later they were still attracted to each other, but now they knew each other well.

Bill told the marriage counselor that he really loved Mary, but it bothered him that she was very indirect sometimes. She was always criticizing him in indirect ways. In fact, he felt afraid of her because he knew she was right sometimes when she criticized him. When she would ask, "Are you going to be home on time tonight?" or, "Don't you think its better to turn your lights on when you drive in the rain?" he knew what she meant. He also knew that a fight could start any time one of these indirect statements came out of her mouth.

Mary also voiced her complaints about Bill to the marriage counselor. "He is so indefinite. Sometimes I feel that I need to give him a multiple choice question to find out what he thinks. You know, sometimes he appears wishy-washy, or weak or perhaps stupid."

In this second vignette, the focus is again on attraction. This time both partners shared goals related to closeness in their relationship, and issues of control appeared as barriers to reaching their goals. The ways in which Bill and Mary expressed their control needs triggered reactions in the partner that seemed opposite of what was hoped for or intended.

* * *

Ned and Lisa had been friends from childhood. They didn't really feel that their relationship had always been very close, but when they found themselves working in the same city and living in the same apartment building, they both decided to renew the relationship.

Lisa knew that her mother would be really excited to learn that she had run into Ned in the big city. When Lisa would show dissatisfaction with a boyfriend, her mother often remarked that she "ought to find a boy just like Ned." Lisa's mother considered Ned perfect son-in-law material, but to Lisa he was just a friend.

Ned really liked Lisa but he felt sure they were friends-not potential lovers or anything else, just friends. While they were growing up he'd always thought of her as a sister. In fact, sometimes he thought of her as a brother. Now that they lived so near each other and neither had other friends, he felt that he was developing a really dependent relationship. He wanted her opinion on almost everything. And she seemed even more dependent on him.

The situation became serious one Friday. Ned returned home from work at about 5:30. He had no plans for the evening. When the phone rang, he wondered who might be calling because he knew no one in the city except Lisa. He heard Lisa's voice ask, "Ned, how about coming to my place for a while? Neither of us knows anyone here, so maybe we should celebrate our first week in the big city.

We could have dinner." Now Ned felt conflicted. Of course he liked her, even loved her in a way, but he thought he should go out to a singles bar or some place to meet other people. "I thought I'd go out for a drink," he said in response to her invitation. Silence. "But you are offering one of your great meals, aren't you?" "We could have some tea and then go to the local bistro together," she said, as if it were a question rather than a suggestion. "OK, We'll go out. You and I are just two kids from the country on the town. I'll be right over," offered Ned.

In the weeks to come, Ned would come to appreciate having a friend in the same apartment building but right now he was trying to figure out a way that he could go out with Lisa and still be able to meet other women. By the time he had reached her apartment he had a clear idea about how to deal with her. After all, weren't they really like sister and brother? Why not just tell people they were siblings?

When Lisa opened her door, she was something to be appreciated. Why couldn't he just think of her as a potential girlfriend? She also was appreciative of him. "Don't you look handsome! I'll bet you don't even care, considering I'm your 'big sister'." He'd forgotten that he had dubbed her that when she tried to be a "boss" back when she turned 18 and he was still only 17. That evening he called her "sis," but she didn't like it much.

At about 6:30, Ned suggested they go out to a nearby bar that he had heard about. He also made his proposition:

"Look, Lisa, why don't we tell people we are brother and sister? That way you can meet some guys and I can meet some women." Lisa didn't seem to like the idea at first, but when Ned told her that from his point of view they really were "just like brother and sister," she agreed.

The bar scene was fun. Many men seemed to approach Lisa, but something about her demeanor discouraged them from getting too close. As Lisa and Ned sat at the bar, a very beautiful woman named Melissa sat next to Ned and started talking to him. Ned didn't know why, but he felt nervous. He felt obligated to tell Melissa that "the lovely girl on my right is my sister. We have just moved here from upstate." "I'll bet, and the bartender is my father," was Melissa's response. "No, I'm not kidding," said Ned. At that point Lisa, who was being psychologically mauled by 3 handsome and dynamic men, turned to Ned. "Let's go, Ned, I don't like the attitude here. It makes me homesick to feel how aggressive and fast everything is here."

Melissa asked Lisa if Ned was really her brother. Lisa said, "Yes, and right now I wish we could go home, in fact I mean all the way back to Morrisville." Melissa then seemed to accept that Ned had really brought his sister to the bar. "You know, I didn't believe you two were sister and brother, but now I can see that you do look alike."

Melissa was clearly interested in Ned, and Lisa realized that the three men after her were all expendable. She didn't like them, so her problem was even more complicated. Ned belonged to her, and she could see no man in the place who was of any concern to her. The only person she had any interest in was Ned. And right now she feared she was about to lose him to Melissa. How could she compete with a sophisticated big city girl with a name to match?

The bad news was that Ned and Melissa were hitting it off. It sounded like they were planning to go somewhere else and to eat dinner together. Ned leaned close to Lisa and told her to grab one of the three men and head out to a little place that Melissa knew about.

Lisa did not want to choose any of these three men. The only man she had any interest in was Ned. And to make matters worse, she had really negative feelings toward Melissa. She did not like her at all. Melissa was too fast for Ned. But what could she do? Lisa decided to appeal to Ned's loyalty to her. "I just don't feel like going out with any of these men. Can't we just stay here for a while and then go home later—maybe have a snack or pizza?"

Ned was taken with Melissa, and he was not about to miss his chance. "Look, I'll bet one of these guys is OK if you give him a chance." Melissa chimed in, "Your problem, Lisa, is that your brother is the most attractive man in this place. These other guys can't measure up."

At that point a miracle seemed to happen. A man walked up to Ned and said, "You lucky devil—two women, and one's your sister. Maybe I can help. My name's Tom. I'm new in town and I don't know anyone. Besides, it took great courage for me to come over here like this. I feel really nervous when I'm talking to a beautiful woman." Lisa found herself instantly attracted to Tom. She thought it was because she felt sorry for him. The four of them went out for dinner and then back to Lisa's apartment where they talked until well after midnight.

In the months that followed the foursome became good friends. It was clear that Melissa and Ned were involved beyond friendship. But Lisa saw Tom as "just another brother," even though she knew Tom wanted more from her.

One afternoon Ned stopped in to see Lisa at work and told her that he needed to talk to her about a big problem he had. After work, Lisa arrived at Ned's apartment. Ned mixed himself a drink and then offered one to Lisa. Lisa didn't drink much but sensed the need for one. "OK, I'll have a little wine." Ned was full of surprises. He wanted to talk about his love affair with Melissa. "She is wonderful in bed," said Ned. Lisa felt consumed by jealousy. "Ned, I don't know if you should tell me everything." "Look, Lisa, you're my big sister. That's the way I think of you, and Melissa thinks you are just that. I am so attracted to her that I don't know what to do. We have great sex, she loves it. But she's a mystery woman. I can't even find out how old she is. I don't know where she lives, works or maybe even what her name is. Her name is supposed to be Melissa Morningstar. Is that real or what? She won't even give me her phone number!"

"It sounds funny to me", said Lisa. To herself she added, "She's married. I like her, but I like Ned, he's mine." Lisa didn't want to share Ned with anyone, least of all Ms. Morningstar. "Maybe she's a vampire or something. Have you ever seen her in the day?" "Come to think of it, I haven't, but I can't accept your vampire theory. You know what the problem is? I'm in love, hypnotized or just crazy about her, and the trouble is the more she frustrates me with this mysterious stuff, the crazier I get. Lisa, I am going to ask her to marry me." Lisa's hand shook and wine spilled on her dress. "I'll be damned." She had never said "damn" before in her life. "Ned, if you marry her I'll die."

Again, attraction is an issue in a friendship between a man and a woman. Issues of jealousy and control are raised here, and appear to interfere with the intimacy level in this friendship when one of the friends is attracted to another person and that new relationship puts limits on the friendship.

These three situations all appear different and yet similar. All three vignettes involve sex because the potential for sexual attraction always appears a possibility. These situations are presented for purposes of examining the behavior and attitudes of the people involved. Awareness of one's own attitudes and behavior can help each of us get more of what we want from our relationships. These three examples form a triangle that mirror all our relationships.

We may consider our relationships as being in one of three arenas: family, friendship, or organizational.

Basic questions are raised that will be relevant for all three of these arenas of human life. We will look at the person in interaction with others in all three of the contexts just presented.

The procedure used in this book is developed fully in the following chapter. The approach will be illustrated in a general way by using the three arenas as a unit for study. We will look at the issues of intimacy and control using the following process:

a. Take a self survey to develop an objective picture of one's attitudes toward others and relationships.

In Chapter 2 we consider concepts such as goals, attitudes, beliefs, assumptions and symbols which are useful in considering how we relate to others.

There are two objectives for Chapter 2: to provide a structure for looking at the specific attitudes the person has in relation to intimacy and control, and to provide a way of thinking about relationships and groups.

b. Develop a picture of the verbal pattern used in conversation with others.

Frameworks presented in Chapter 3 may be used to gain a perspective on the ways one communicates with others. Procedures are presented which help people think about the kinds of intimacy and control messages they send to others.

c. Practice methods for conversation analysis.

In Chapter 4, ways of using the structures for analyzing intimacy and control elements in conversations are presented. Attention is given to both interaction with others and the kinds of messages that may be thought of as what we say to ourselves, "self talk."

d. Use structured experience for practicing desired behavior.

The emphasis in Chapter 5 is on development and practice of specific patterns of talk that you want to include in your talking repertoire.

This chapter includes ideas for practicing new elements you would like to incorporate into your speech pattern. Suggestions, hints, and tips are included as well as an overall framework that can be used as a sort of guide if you desire to develop your own structured experiences.

e. Consider nonverbal behavior patterns.

Chapter 6 provides ideas for thinking about the nonverbal aspects of our behavior, the messages sent by our bodies rather than by the words we speak.

Often they are more important than the words themselves. The purpose of this chapter is to provide ways of thinking about and gaining control of the nonverbal messages we send to others.

f. Seek out the relationship with the self.

This emphasis is presented in Chapter 7 but it is not necessarily the last step. The five steps in the process are more a circular process than a linear one. For example, after looking at the self relationship one might simply go back to step 1, and consider one's attitudes.

The assumptions made by the authors are that when we look at our selves in relation to others, we usually focus on some signal that could be in the form of an idea, problem, feeling, question or opinion. Something gets our attention.

In each of three vignettes presented in this chapter, issues of intimacy and control were raised. In subsequent chapters we provide a method for shedding light on three questions that were raised by the three examples:

1.How does the level of intimacy influence the level of control I have in a relationship?

2.How does the way I express control influence the level of intimacy in a relationship?

3.How does the level of intimacy in a relationship change with changes in my feelings about control?

CHAPTER 2

Foundations of Intimacy and Control Behaviors: How Do We Think About Intimacy and Control?

What Do We Want From Intimacy and Control?

When we enter into a relationship, intimacy and control are among the most important issues we will need to consider: how close to be, and how to exercise control in the relationship.

These two great human issues seem always with us in our contacts with others. In our more involved and lasting relations, whether focused on friendship, work or love, these two key elements appear to dominate our concerns.

Several questions will be used to focus our attention on these issues:

- *What do we want and expect from a close relationship?*
- *What are our attitudes toward control and intimacy?*
- *How are these attitudes related to one another?*
- *What barriers exist that affect these relationships?*

Consideration of these questions helps us understand our face to face relationships.

We have chosen to look at our goals, attitudes, perceptions and behaviors to describe our relationships in terms of intimacy and control. Finally, how can we describe our goals, attitudes and assumptions about intimacy and control? These questions form the focus for our discussion.

Our ideas and experiences of intimacy and control in social interaction do suggest answers to these questions. Information (data) we have collected provides a basis for speculating about these relationships.

In this discussion about the relationship between intimacy and control we shall try to make it clear when we move from a description of what we systematically observe to speculation based on individual experience.

Goals, Expectations, Attitudes, Assumptions and Symbols

At some level the use of these words is confused and confusing. Perhaps this is reasonable considering the overlapping meaning of many words and ideas that we use to characterize our relationships. Consider the following statement made by a man who is about to marry:

"I want to settle down and have a real friend (my wife to be), someone I can share my feelings, thoughts and experiences with. I expect to have and want to have a really close relationship. That's what a marriage is—two people who can share, trust, enjoy and grow in appreciation of one another."

This statement provides an example of each of those words that are basic to the understanding of this chapter.

This person has a *goal* in mind for the relationship, stated in terms of what he wants. The statement itself offers some detail about the type of relationship he wants with the person he is planning to marry.

In this case the *expectation* is apparently closely linked to the *goal*. The person expects to achieve the goal. That is, it is his *expectation* that the type of relationship he wants will exist when the marriage occurs. He is clearly making certain *assumptions* about the intended partner, and perhaps about marriage itself. The assumptions are closely related to his expectations; he assumes certain qualities are characteristic of his future wife and marriage, and therefore expects that certain things will happen in the marriage.

The person's attitudes toward relationships and specifically intimacy are also clear. An *attitude* may be thought of as a predisposition to act, or a way of thinking and feeling about something, similar to a belief. The person's attitude toward intimacy can be described as positive, at least in the context of marriage.

The *symbol* is important because it is often thought of as what we want, but may merely stand for what we are really trying to achieve.

In the situation presented, marriage could represent the desired relationship, and in that sense marriage is the symbol.

The following material and exercises are designed to help the reader gain an understanding of how goals, expectations, assumptions, attitudes and symbols influence our relationships.

In general, people seem to want and expect two things from a relationship: to be treated fairly, and to be close. In other words, our relationship goals, or what we personally want from relationships, lie mainly in the areas of intimacy and control. Often we understand these goals more in terms of symbols than in the reality of intimacy or control. To many, marriage is more a symbol of intimacy than the real thing.

People do seek intimacy and control in their relationships with others. Often the search is not for power over a person or closeness to a person, but rather for achievement of the symbols of power or intimacy. The goals that people expect to attain in relationships seem as many and varied as the number of relationships in the world.

What do we expect and want from a relationship? Some common goals are stated in terms of intimacy. Think about some of the statements people make about what they want in life:

"I want to be married"

"I want to share my life with another person"

"I want a good family"

"I want to have *support* from someone in a close relationship"

"I want a good sexual relationship"

"I want companionship - I fear loneliness"

"I want an attractive lover"

"I want a physical relationship - lots of touching"

"I want to be accepted as I am"

"I want someone to tell my troubles to"

These are some common goals people try to achieve in relationships, as well as many of the satisfactions people expect in their closest relationships.

What kinds of power and control do we want and expect in our relationships? People do need, want and expect power and control over their lives, and see close relationships as having something to do with getting what they want. Consider the following types of statements:

"I want to feel confident"

"I would like not to have to worry about money"

"I want to get a good education"

"I want to have the necessary things for the good life"

"I don't want demands placed on me"

"I want to feel important"

"I want to have a good job"

"I want to feel that when I compete I win"

"I want to be strong"

"I want to be treated fairly and to be equal"

Probably you have some items you could add to the list of statements related to power and control.

The point of presenting such specific issues is to show that most of us do want and expect rather specific outcomes from relationships. Also, we can see from these lists that what we want and expect is easily thought of in two general categories, Intimacy and Control.

One easy exercise to focus attention on a relationship is to *share expectations*. This exercise may be used in any relationship - a close relationship like a marriage, a friendship, a family relationship (parent-child), or a work relationship. Results of the exercises may pinpoint a problem which represents an area for growth in the relationship.

Exercise: What are our expectations?

To increase the potential success of the experience, certain steps can be helpful. First, accept the other's statement of expectation-do not judge or criticize it. Yours may seem as inappropriate to your partner as his/hers does to you. Second, be sure you understand one another's expectations clearly. Be sure to *restate* one anothers' expectations and check to be sure they are commonly understood. Third, try to see if each person understands the other's reason for having the expectation.

This process is perhaps the most time-consuming activity. During this activity it is important to *listen carefully.* Use frequent paraphrasing of the other's statements. Ask questions if necessary for understanding.

1.Write a short statement about what you want from your relationship with.... (A person with whom you have a relationship).

2.List five separate but important expectations.

3.Rank the 5 expectations of importance to you.

4. After both you and the other person have completed steps 1, 2, and 3, share your lists with each other.

5. Notice agreements and disagreements. Also discuss any items that appear on one list but not the other.

6. Now discuss the following specific issues: What can we agree on as a next step for resolving any discrepancy, difference or conflict that was raised as a result of the exercise? Choose something for resolution that you both feel you have a reasonably good chance to achieve.

Are Our Symbols Real?

Closely related to our goals for intimacy and control are the *symbols* that represent the actual goals. No one really feels that symbols alone produce happiness, but often the symbol is pursued as though it were the actual goal.

Sometimes the goal and symbol can be combined. Perhaps the best example is marriage. Marriage may be thought of as a symbol of intimacy. Often people will ask others, "Are you married?" Another way of asking this question might be, "Are you involved in an intimate relationship that would put limits on any close relationship I might have with you?"

Symbols for power are well known. Perhaps the most important is money. Of course money is not only a symbol but in most circumstances it is also the instrument of power. This may be most clearly expressed by the phrase "everyone has his price," which implies that if you have enough money you can control anyone.

Often it is the symbol that we seek, and confuse the symbol with the goal. When we get it we realize that the symbol was not what we wanted, but only represented something we wanted or thought we wanted.

We define a symbol of intimacy or control as something (an object, idea, person, relationship) that represents the goal. The goal is to meet our needs for closeness to another, or needs to control the self and/or the life environment.

So a symbol is not what the person really wants, but is seen as having some very basic connection with the real goal. If I feel lonely, marriage may be my symbol for closeness as well as my goal. I may want to have certain opportunities. Money will allow me to live where I wish and do what I want. I may think that I will be in control of my life if I have enough money. I can get others to do what I want if I have money. In this way the symbol is also the instrument to reach the specific goal. I want to control my life, my social environment, so with enough money I can live where and how I want.

Some common symbols of intimacy are marriage, a ring, a bed, a kiss, an embrace and a gift. Symbols of power include money, awards, big cars, gavels, firm handshakes, loud voices, and a clenched fist. Some symbols of intimacy may also be seen as symbols of control. The reverse does not appear to be true.

How do you use symbols of intimacy and control in talking to others? Do you tell people you are happily married to a wealthy doctor? That your wife turned down a promotion so she could spend more time with you? Or talk about letters from your son, the champion athlete and scholar?

To get more of a feeling for how we use symbols, imagine two young men talking about the important symbols in their lives:

"How are things going?"

"Great! I got all A's last semester, and also I've met someone I am very serious about."

"Nice going. I got a little promotion at work, myself. It's not anything real big yet, but I think I'm on my way. Not a lot of money so far, but I did get a change of title — Assistant Sales Manager."

[Time passes]

"Hey, how's it been? (Spoken heartily, with a firm handshake.)

"Well, remember what I said about that woman I met and liked?"

"Sure."

"We're engaged."

"All right! You're getting to be a regular settled man!"

We assume these young men find satisfaction in the symbols of intimacy and control they spoke of. But another person may wonder why getting what he wants rarely results in feelings of satisfaction, accomplishment or happiness. Perhaps the achievement of a symbol must remain what it is and nothing more: the achievement of a representation of what you really want.

One way to look at what you want from a relationship is to consider what you want, and think about whether or not your goal is actually a symbol or representation of the intimacy and/or control you really want.

Exercise: What are your symbols?

Try the following exercise: First, partners individually write down at least ten and no more than fifteen things you want in your life. Then rank them in descending order of importance from things you want most to least. After both you and your partner have finished the ranking, then come together and talk about your items. Focus discussion on the following:

1.Any items that you both share in common. Talk about what they mean to each of you.

2.Differences in the symbols that each of you have used.

3.Items that you both seem particularly interested in discussing.

4.Any items that seem to be related to conflicts you have.

5.Any other items you wish to discuss.

A Directionality Model

One way to think about power or control is to think of "higher" as more powerful and "lower" as less powerful. The language reflects this idea. Examples exist in everything we might think about.

Children are told to look up to parents — and in fact children do physically look up to parents.

- *We all start at the bottom but may work our way up.*
- *We are told not to look down on those who are less fortunate.*
- *Many people try to get to the top of their organization.*
- *Some people are upwardly mobile.*

We are also inclined to think about intimacy in terms of *distance,* closer or farther:

- *"I feel very distant."*
- *"The more we spend time together the closer we become."*
- *"I do not feel close when we're apart."*
- *"Your voice sounds like you are somewhere else."*
- *"We are very close to one another."*

Throughout this book we use a simple model to illustrate the way many people think and talk about intimacy and control. Intimacy and control can both be described in terms of *subjectively experienced distance:* How far from or close to you do I feel? How far above or below you do I feel?

In this model intimacy and control may be illustrated by two lines, horizontal for intimacy and vertical for control.

Responsive Control

If we think about our own attitudes and those of others we know, it seems that our closest relationships could be pictured in the upper and lower left quadrants - areas of greater levels of intimacy and of directive to responsive control (A and C). Most people desire closeness and equality, under certain conditions. The attitudes we hold toward the interaction of intimacy and control could be expressed as, "If I let myself be known to others, I will lose some of my power with them. When people know me I will be vulnerable and thus weakened." Of course, the theme of this expression is, "I'm not sure of myself." Getting to know someone involves revealing and finding out about weaknesses and other aspects of the self thought not to be good. Attitudes of caution about closeness and desire for power over others we can picture in the upper right quadrant (B). Using the diagram as an aid to understanding, we can see that attitudes located in quadrants B and D exist primarily in relationships where intimacy is seen as disadvantageous or unproductive. Superior-subordinate relationships within organizational structures characterized by clear hierarchical distinctions (military and religious organizations, for example) are usually located in quadrant B. Many work and business relationships in less well-defined structures would fall in area D.

We are suggesting that in egalitarian relationships attitudes of wanting closeness are related to the desire to share power with others. The stronger the attitude toward being close, the stronger is the inclination toward sharing power. For example, one might say, "I want to be close and I know that I can't be close if I try to control the other person, so I must share decisions with that other person," or "I want to control the other person so I cannot afford to be too intimate. If I am intimate I will be vulnerable."

Many of our strongest resistances toward intimacy have to do with being careful, cautious, and suspicious. It is fairly clear that as a person becomes concerned with having control, he or she will also increase defenses against closeness.

We will now take a look at some specific ways of examining attitudes toward intimacy and control in our lives.

There is much evidence in the fields of applied psychology that supports the idea that control and intimacy are related. As people move closer, they may become more vulnerable. As people feel out of control, they may create distance in their relationships.

Check yourself on some of your own thoughts about intimacy and control. The diagram presents a framework for thinking about these attitudes. Simply ask yourself where you think you want to locate yourself. Of course, most of us have thoughts, feelings, and attitudes that fall in the middle of these scales. It does help to think of our own specific reactions, what they are like, how they change, and how thoughts about intimacy are related to those about control.

The following exercise is designed to help partners in a relationship clarify their attitudes toward intimacy and control and to compare their perceptions of one another's attitudes.

Exercise: How Close Is Up Or Down?

In this exercise, each partner responds for him/herself and for the other. Think about your attitudes toward relationships such as one finds in marriage. Also think about how your partner feels about that close relationship. Some important attitudes about relationships are contained in the following statements. First answer each statement for yourself, by putting a check (✓) in the appropriate place. Then answer each item the way you think your partner would answer. That is, if your partner were very frank about his/her attitudes, this is the way he/she would respond. Then designate this reaction with an ✗ in the appropriate place.

YES NO

❑ ❑ 1. I like to share decisions in a relationship.

❑ ❑ 2. I like to feel equal in a relationship.

❑ ❑ 3. I can feel as equal with a woman as with a man.

❑ ❑ 4. I want to dominate my partner in a sexual relationship.

❑ ❑ 5. My commitment to myself prevents me from giving control to others.

❑ ❑ 6. I like to tell others what to do.

❑ ❑ 7. In a close relationship people don't listen carefully to each other.

❑ ❑ 8. Each person has a personal space which must be defended so that others do not come too close.

❑ ❑ 9. I tend to distrust people who are concerned with closeness and intimacy.

❑ ❑ 10. I like to share my thoughts and feelings with my partner.

❑ ❑ 11. I receive my greatest satisfaction through really intimate relationships.

❑ ❑ 12. When I become intimate with another I reduce the possibility of being manipulated or rejected.

After you have completed the scale you can compute scores for yourself and your partner. Your partner's score is based on how you thought she/he would respond. For an intimacy score, award a 2 for every *yes* response for items 10, 11, and 12; a 2 for each *no* on items, 7, 8, and 9. Do this for yourself and for your partner. A control score is calculated by awarding a 2 for a *yes* to items 1, 2, and 3; and a 2 for each *no* on items 4, 5, and 6. Compute one for your partner also.

1.Compare your score with the score you gave your partner.

2.The higher the intimacy score, the more "intimacy-oriented" are your attitudes; the higher the control score, the more "equality-oriented" are your attitudes.

3.Now share your reactions with your partner.

Attitudes

The diagram on the next page is the same basic model we have presented before. Here, however, we have added some statements that seem typical of attitudes, beliefs or assumptions that would be represented by the four quadrants of the figure.

If we think about relationships which exist at the extremes of the intimacy and control dimensions, we can predict certain interactive styles which are consistent with the attitudes described in the figure.

WHAT ARE YOUR ATTITUDES?

DIRECTIVE CONTROL

Overly critical of those close
No need to listen
Concern with being in charge
Concern with being in control
Concern with having your way

A

B

CLOSENESS

Like to feel close
Enjoy intimate relationships
Express feelings & thoughts
Take risks to increase intimacy
Share deep feelings

DISTANCE

Not too close
Few people want intimacy
Closeness involves conflicts
Personal space must be defended
Loss of individuality

RESPONSIVE CONTROL

Listen to others
Accept other people
Share control
Trust & respect others
Encourage others to participate

C

D

A: Includes relationships characterized by high degrees of directive control and emotional closeness. People who are in this space have attitudes like good old-fashioned parents and teachers — strict but loving.

In a family setting, members would place a high value on taking very good care of one another emotionally and physically, and pay a lot of attention to each other. Thoughts and feelings are shared freely, but overtly or subtly each family member has to do what the parent in authority wants. Expectations are predictable, and support feelings of security in each member.

B: Includes relationships based on high directive control and great emotional distance. In this space people are emotionally neutral and controlling with one another. A couple in this situation may live a well-ordered life without much warmth or directly-expressed emotion. One of them usually is the formal "boss," though the other may be manipulative to get his/her way. In work relationships, people would tend to avoid personal involvement with one another, and to respond primarily to directive leadership from persons in authority.

C: Relationships in this space are characterized by equality and emotional closeness. Such relationships tend to be seen as unusual and special. Couples and families tend to see periods of time in which their relationships existed in this area as "the best times." Maintenance of ongoing relationships in this space requires consistent work at developing communication skills.

D: Relationships characterized by great equality and emotional neutrality. Juries, technical and professional teams operating in a democratic shared decision making model would be included here.

How Important are the Assumptions we hold about Intimacy and Control?

One thing we all have in common is that throughout our lives we receive important messages about intimacy and control. Some we believe, articulate and act on. Others do not seem to influence us. There is a group of commonly understood assumptions about intimacy and control that most of us know in some form.

For intimacy, some of the most widely held assumptions include:

1. Intimacy breeds contempt.
2. Intimacy means pain.
3. Happiness is not possible without intimacy.
4. Self disclosure will produce intimacy.
5. People fear intimacy.
6. We are most intimate with people (strangers) we will never meet again.

7. Intimate relationships are always sexual.

8. The deepest intimacy can only occur between people of the same sex.

9. Revealing "secrets" makes people feel more intimate.

10. Revealing "secret fears or weakness" results in rejection.

11. Intimacy is based on common interest.

12. Real intimacy cannot exist with a superior or subordinate.

13. One loses individuality in intimate relationships.

14. One can be intimate with anything, not just people.

15. Intimacy produces conflict.

16. Most intimate relationships are produced in a dark place.

17. We are all really alone.

18. There is no way for a person to control his/her attractions. It's "chemistry."

19. People need space — it's natural.

20. Satisfaction in a relationship depends on finding the right person.

21. People have needs for privacy.

22. When people know each other too well all the excitement goes out of a relationship.

23. People can only become intimate with their "own kind."

24. Intimacy is the greatest happiness of life.

25. Intimacy with those closest to us is the secret of happiness and effectiveness.

26. Mutually intimate conversation would solve many work and human relations problems.

27. Intimate interaction has a positive "ripple effect" on all other more formal human interactions.

28. A person expands in energy and feelings of worth in an intimate relationship.

29. Intimacy is natural for people; to be distant is artificial.

30. God is intimate with his Creation.

31. Intimacy produces natural power.

32. Children develop best in an atmosphere that includes a lot of intimacy.

33. Intimacy with one's self is the key to all other intimacies.

34. Intimacy is the secret of the universe.

We also send and receive messages about power and control. We all hold assumptions about power. These assumptions act as continuing message senders to all of us. Some common assumptions about power or control held by many of us are:

1. Power corrupts and absolute power corrupts absolutely.

2. One member of a relationship has to be dominant.

3. Everyone needs to be told what to do once in a while.

4. In order to get things done someone has to be in charge.

5. People who have power deserve respect.

6. Men are strong and women are weak.

7. In order to learn we need structure.

8. Some people need a "kick in the pants" to get things done.

9. Children need limits.

10. Committees can't really get any work done.

11. Human nature is basically selfish and it won't change.

12. Everyone is out to get as much power as possible for himself.

13. Everyone has the potential to become "power mad."

14. Some one person must always make the final decision.

15. It is better to take the wrong action than do nothing.

16. Democracy works well in theory. In practice we need a strong leader.

17. Men are better leaders than women.

18. We are really not equal in anything.

19. In all relations someone must be the dependent person.

20. Power is given to certain special people.

21. Equality is an illusion.

22. It is important to question authority.

23. If people become too trusting, one person will take advantage of the other.

24. Inner control brings order and beauty to a person's outer life.

25. To mutually influence one another is a very happy situation.

26. Control frees us from anarchy *and* domination.

27. Powerlessness is a terrible condition. It is natural to want power, influence and control.

28. There is an unlimited supply of power and control; one need not take others'.

29. To have power with others is a wonderful thing.

30. The cure for an ailing democracy is more democracy.

31. Democracy hasn't been tried and found wanting, it simply hasn't been fairly tried.

32. A group working on a problem has more intelligence and knowledge than the same people working alone.

33. Small groups make us what we are in life.

34. God sometimes just waits quietly.

These comprehensive lists of commonly held assumptions about intimacy and control have been presented to assist you in identification of your own assumptions.

Although none of these assumptions represents a theme for intimacy or control that everyone accepts, they do indicate some of the messages that we have been exposed to.

The themes of these messages seem to represent rather extreme points of view. Many suggest the fears associated with extremes: "Someone needs to be in control or it won't work" and "One needs to be careful about sharing himself or hurt will result."

Exercise: What can we assume about our assumptions? How important to you are your assumptions?

The following exercise provides an opportunity to explore your assumptions with another person.

1. What assumptions do *you* have about intimacy and control? List two for control and two for intimacy.

2. Now choose from *our* lists 3 assumptions for intimacy and 3 for control that you like and react to positively.

3. Share your list and selections with your partner (or other person(s) with you). In your discussion see how your and your partner's assumptions are similar and different.

Intimacy Attitude Scale

We find out through our own experience that we hold many assumptions about relationships. This work is about getting control of your behavior so you can get what you want. Behavior is an expression of a belief or attitudinal system that is grounded in assumptions. Now we will look at specific attitudes that we hold toward closeness, intimacy and trust.

Our investigation of assumptions held about intimacy has led to the development of an instrument, the Intimacy Attitude Scale (IAS), which yields measures of specific ways people say they feel about close relationships.

Now that you have focused attention on your assumptions about intimacy, complete the 31 items of the IAS and score it for yourself.

INTIMACY ATTITUDE SCALE

The following items reflect feelings and attitudes that people have toward others and relationships with others. Specifically the items are concerned with attitudes of closeness, intimacy and trust. We would like you to respond in the following way: Please rate each of the following items on a scale of 1 to 9, so that 1 represents strong *disagreement* and 9 represents strong *agreement*. Do this by placing the appropriate number 1-9 before (on the left) all of the items.Use the following scale as a guideline.

[ ] 1. My concern with rejection inhibits my expression of feelings to others.

[ ] 2. I'm concern with being dominated in a close relationship with another.

[ ] 3. I'm often overly critical of people in a close relationship.

[ ] 4. I will tell a person my feelings if I feel very attracted to him/her.

[ ] 5. I want to feel close to people I really like and will reveal my deepest feelings to them.

[ ] 6. I would rather not be too close because it usually involves conflict.

[ ] 7. When I feel attracted to a person, I want to seek out a close relationship.

[ ] 8. People receive their greatest satisfaction through really intimate relationships.

[ ] 9. I personally search for close intimate relationships.

[ ] 10. I would like to be able to form close relationships easily.

[ ] 11. I want to be able to share my feelings and thoughts with others.

[ ] 12. I often want to talk with someone about my feelings toward another person with whom I am in a close relationship.

[ ] 13. Each person has a personal space that must be defended so others do not come too close.

[ ] 14. I tend to distrust people who are concerned with closeness and intimacy.

[ ] 15. I have concerns about losing my individuality in close relationships.

[ ] 16. People must give up control if they enter into a really intimate relationship.

[ ] 17. Being honest and open with another person makes both people feel closer to one another.

[ ] 18. If I were another person I would be interested in getting to know me.

[ ] 19. Revealing secrets about my sex life makes me feel close to others.

[ ] 20. Generally I can feel just as close to a woman as I can to a man.

[ ] 21. It's easier for me to be intimate with other people when I am in a place of natural beauty.

[ ] 22. I want to be sure that I am in good control before I attempt to become intimate with another person.

[ ] 23. My commitments to people prevent me from becoming intimate with other people.

[ ] 24. Undressing with members of a group can lead to an increased level of intimacy.

[ ] 25. I think that people who want to become intimate have hidden reasons for wanting closeness.

[ ] 26. When I become intimate with another I reduce the possibility of being manipulated by that other person.

[ ] 27. Intimacy and sex are related but one can exist without the other.

[ ] 28. Sex and intimacy are the same and one cannot exist without the other.

[ ] 29. I can be most intimate in a physical sexual relationship.

[ ] 30. The demands placed on me by those with whom I have intimate relationships often inhibit my own need satisfaction.

[ ] 31. I understand and accept that intimacy leads to bad feelings as well as good feelings.

Three scores will be computed: a positive, a negative and a total score.

1. First, place a minus (-) before your rating of each of the 14 negative items. Negative items are 1, 2, 3, 6, 13, 14, 15, 16, 21, 22, 23, 25, 28 and 30.

2. Next, place a plus (+) before your rating of each of the 17 positive items. Positive items are 4, 5, 7, 8, 9, 10, 11, 12, 17, 18, 19, 20, 24, 26, 27, 29 and 31.

3. Add all the positive ratings. There should be 17 positive ratings. The total of all 17 ratings is your positive score.

4. Add all the negative ratings. There should be 14 negative ratings. The total of all 14 ratings is your negative score.

5. Calculate your total score by subtracting the negative score from the positive score.

EXAMPLE:

Positive score = 94

Negative score = 60

Total score = 34

We are interested in looking carefully at how our attitudes are related to the attitudes of others, what they are like and what specific elements are included in positive, negative and overall attitudes toward intimacy.

The positive intimacy score could perhaps be best expressed as:

"The degree to which the person wants to share feelings, ideas and experiences, honestly and openly in sexual and nonsexual relationships."

The negative intimacy score could be described as:

"The degree to which the person is concerned with domination, conflict, criticism, freedom, distrust, and powerlessness in close relationships whether sexual or nonsexual."

There are 17 items in the positive scale, therefore a score of 85 represents the midpoint for the positive scale items. If you feel that you scored lower than you thought you would, or "should" have, look at those items you disagreed with (any item you rated below 5) and think about the specific issue raised by that item.

When analyzing one's "scores" and reactions to items, it is extremely useful to have opportunities for discussion with a partner or small group of people.

The negative scale is handled the same way as the positive. Since there are 14 items, a score of 70 indicates an average item score of 5 (neutral). A score above 70 means that your reaction generally is resistant to being close. A lower score would indicate less resistance to intimacy.

The total score represents your overall attitude toward intimacy. Recall that the total score is derived by subtracting your negative score (fear of, resistance to intimacy) from your positive score (desire for, drive toward intimacy) and in this sense represents the balance between these two opposing forces.

You can compare all three of your scores. What can you find out? Are you very high or low on any of the three scales? Is there a pattern to your scores? If you are high on total scores because you have a very high positive score and a high negative score, it's different from having the same high total score but with medium positive score and a very low negative score. It's worthwhile to study your own pattern and then see where you are in relationship to the information presented in the following chart.

Your positive score reflects your desire for intimacy and your negative score your resistance to intimacy. Your total score is indicates your desire for intimacy as modified by your resistance to intimacy.

In a number of studies Intimacy Attitude Scale scores have been found to be positively related to other measures of intimacy, openness, trust, and self disclosure. As our discussion of positive and negative scores suggests, this total score has little meaning by itself in the individual case. It is possible to make statements about the meaning of the total score only when a large number of cases is considered.

You can get an idea of your own pattern of attitudes toward intimacy by looking at the Patterns of Attitudes table.

PATTERNS OF ATTITUDES
Comparison of Combinations

Hi Pos 119 -153	Hi Pos 119 -153	Hi Pos 119 -153
Hi Neg 98 -126	Med Neg 45 - 97	Lo Neg 14 - 44
	***	
Med Pos 52 -118	Med Pos 52 -118	Med Pos 52 -118
Hi Neg 98 -126	Med Neg 45 - 97	Lo Neg 14 - 44
	***	
Lo Pos 17 - 51	Lo Pos 17 - 51	Lo Pos 17 - 51
Hi Neg 28 - 126	Med Neg 45 - 97	Lo Neg 14 - 44
	***	
TOTAL		
Hi =104 - 153	Med = 35 - 103	Lo = 0 - 34

The Hi, Hi condition is characterized by a strong desire to be close with extensive concerns about possible problems in close relationships.

The Hi, Med condition suggests a point of view of wanting close relationships, feeling positive about intimacy and having some concern about problems that might be involved.

The Hi, Lo combination indicates a person who feels positively toward close relations and has little concern about problems in these relationships.

The Med, Hi type could be described as having some positive attitudes toward intimacy with much distrust and resistance regarding close relationships.

The person with a Med, Med range score has some positive attitudes toward intimacy, and some resistance to it.

The Med, Lo person has some positive attitudes toward close relations and little resistance. The Lo, Hi combination means little desire to be close and great distrust of and concern with close relationships.

The Lo, Med combination has little desire for intimacy combined with some concerns about control in intimate relationships.

The Lo, Lo type expresses little desire for intimacy and little resistance as well.

Do you want the set of attitudes you have? How does your pattern of attitudes differ from your ideal? Do you want to change? Try to think about it descriptively: That's the way I am, feel, react, think, believe.

The Control Attitude Scale (CAS) is identical to the IAS in form; it has the same number of items and uses the same scoring procedure.

Continue this process of investigating your own attitudes by completing the CAS.

CONTROL ATTITUDE SCALE

The following items reflect feelings and attitudes that people have toward others, and relationships with others. Specifically the items are concerned with attitudes toward power, control and authority. We would like you to respond in the following way: Please rate each of the following items on a scale of 1 to 9, so that 1 represents strong *disagreement* and 9 represents strong *agreement.* Do this by placing the appropriate number 1-9 before (on the left) all of the items.

Use the following scale as a guideline.

[ ] 1. Concern about my status in the group inhibits me in expressing suggestions to others.

[ ] 2. I'm concerned with my ability to control my own behavior in relationships with others.

[ ] 3. I'm often overly directive with people.

[ ] 4. I will listen to and accept the ideas of another person with whom I have a relationship.

[ ] 5. I want to feel equal to others in relationships or groups.

[ ] 6. I would rather not have any control in a relationship.

[ ] 7. When a person listens to me I feel less need to dominate the conversation.

[ ] 8. I am always the way I want to be in a relationship.

[ ] 9. I search for relationships that are equal and reciprocal.

[ ] 10. I would like to be able to be the way I really want to be.

[ ] 11. I can control myself and if I want to let go I can.

[ ] 12. I often am concerned about my own decision making process.

[ ] 13. In relations, people should maintain individual control for decisions.

[ ] 14. I tend to distrust people who believe in equality and reciprocity in relationships.

[ ] 15. I have concern about losing my control over myself and my life in relationships.

[ ] 16. In a work relationship, people must give up closeness with each other.

[ ] 17. I know that if I want to do something I will be able to do it.

[ ] 18. I am not perceived as domineering.

[ ] 19. I want to dominate my partner in a sexual relationship.

[ ] 20. Generally I can feel just as equal with women as I can with men.

[ ] 21. It's easier for me to feel equal in a relationship when I am in informal surroundings.

[ ] 22. I want to be sure that I am very close in a relationship before I give up trying to control the other person.

[ ] 23. My commitment to myself prevents me from giving up control to others.

[ ] 24. If I really want to do something, I know I can do it.

[ ] 25. I think people who want equality in relationships have hidden reasons for wanting it.

[ ] 26. By developing equality in a relationship with another person, I reduce the possibility of being rejected.

[ ] 27. I trust myself to develop appropriate relationships with other people.

[ ] 28. I am in control of my life and not interested in trying to control others.

[ ] 29. I feel comfortable not having the control in a relationship.

[ ] 30. I can control myself and I can also let go.

[ ] 31. I know that equality in a relationship leads to conflict as well as cooperation.

The positive items are 4, 5, 7, 8, 9, 10, 11, 17, 18, 20, 24, 26, 27, 28, 29, 30, and 31. The negative items for the Control Attitude Scale are 1, 2, 3, 6, 12, 13, 14, 15, 16, 19, 21, 22, 23, and 25.

Refer back to the scoring and interpretation section on the Intimacy Attitude Scale (p. 55-56) to guide your analysis and thinking of your responses to the Control Attitude Scale.

The positive scale score reflects attitudes toward egalitarian relationships. A person with a high positive scale score could be described as seeking equality in relationships.

The negative scale score indicates the desire for relationships which are directive, that is, someone is in charge or one person has more control in the relationship.

How Do You Think About Your Own Behavior?

We have examined feelings and attitudes toward and reactions to the issues of intimacy and control in relationships. Now we will focus on behavior — the way we act and what we say to others in conversation.

How intimate is your behavior with others? An instrument, the Intimacy Orientation Technique (IOT), has been developed to sharpen a person's perception of his/her own conversational behavior. The 30 IOT items provide a broad index of a person's behavioral tendencies.

Now complete the 30 IOT items to gain another perspective on your orientation toward intimacy.

THE INTIMACY ORIENTATION TECHNIQUE

Imagine yourself in the company of another person or persons with whom you have a relationship. Choose the response for each item that seems to best describe your behavior, and check (✓) the letter which precedes that response.

1. You are thinking about how to start the conversation; you would probably

   ☐ a. say nothing, just listen (1)

   ☐ b. tell how you feel (10)

   ☐ c. relate your feelings in other situations (7)

   ☐ d. ask people to relate what they know about groups in general (3)

2. You are talking about goals; you would probably

   ☐ a. say that everyone needs goals (3)

   ☐ b. share an observation of what you see happening in the relationship (9)

   ☐ c. remind the other person of a previous time when the same subject was discussed (6)

   ☐ d. relate your feelings about not having a goal (10)

3. You are concerned about some people close to both (all) of you; you would probably

- ☐ a. relate the appropriate psychology theory (3)
- ☐ b. express your feelings toward people in another group to which you belong (7)
- ☐ c. express your feelings toward the person(s) with you (10)
- ☐ d. change the subject (2)

4. Authority seems to be an issue in your relationship; you would probably

- ☐ a. relate your feelings about another group you are in (7)
- ☐ b. comment on the role of person(s) you are with (9)
- ☐ c. express your feelings toward authorities you have known (7)
- ☐ d. bring up similar events from past discussions (6)

5. The topic seems to be reactions to strong emotions; you would probably

- ☐ a. tell how you feel when you are with other friends (7)
- ☐ b. tell how you feel toward the person with whom you are talking (10)
- ☐ c. start discussing emotions in relationships and groups (3)
- ☐ d. change the topic (2)

6. The topic is sexual issues; you would probably

- ☐ a. talk about how people deal with the topic of sex (3)
- ☐ b. relate your feelings to those you are with (10)
- ☐ c. tell about your feelings about sex in other relationships (7)
- ☐ d. remind the person(s) of a discussion on the same topic in the past (6)

7. The conversation seems to have violent tone; you would probably

- ☐ a. tell how you are feeling (10)
- ☐ b. point out that violence exists in all groups (3)
- ☐ c. talk about conflicts you have resolved in the past (6)
- ☐ d. say nothing and hope the subject changes (1)

8. You are talking about some activities you could do together; you would probably

- ☐ a. say that you wish you could express your feelings (8)
- ☐ b. express your feelings about the activities (10)
- ☐ c. relate how people use activities to meet the need of getting closer (3)
- ☐ d. tell how you share confidences with others (4)

9. In a period of uncomfortable silence, you would probably

- ☐ a. wait to hear how the other person(s) react (1)
- ☐ b. express your feelings about the silence (10)
- ☐ c. share your observations about what's happening here (9)
- ☐ d. say that the group has had periods of silence in the past (6)

10. You are talking about how close you want to be to each other; you would probably

- ☐ a. tell how you feel about getting close to the other person (10)
- ☐ b. tell that you had decided to sit quietly (9)
- ☐ c. tell how you feel about being close to other persons (7)
- ☐ d. tell that you have discussed this issue with another person (4)

11. You are talking about the weather; you would probably

- ☐ a. continue the discussion (2)
- ☐ b. tell how you feel about the discussion (10)
- ☐ c. tell how you think the weather affects your relationship (9)
- ☐ d. tell how the weather influences your feelings toward your (other) friends (7)

12. You seem to be avoiding an important issue; you would probably

- ☐ a. talk about the tendency of people to avoid painful issues (3)
- ☐ b. make an observation on present behavior (9)
- ☐ c. tell how you deal with difficult issues with your (other) friends (7)
- ☐ d. express your feelings about the discussion (10)

13. The/a person you are with has just told you that he/she is attracted to you; you would probably

- ☐ a. express your feelings at that moment (10)
- ☐ b. talk about interpersonal attraction (3)
- ☐ c. say that he/she seems to feel free to express feelings (9)
- ☐ d. tell about feelings you have had toward others (7)

14. You are talking about fears of being hurt in a relationship; you would probably

- ☐ a. talk about fear in groups (3)
- ☐ b. relate times this has occurred before in this relationship (6)
- ☐ c. talk about your feelings about being hurt by others (7)
- ☐ d. describe how you have dealt with this with other friends (4)

15. You are talking about leaders; you would probably

- ☐ a. change the subject of the discussion (2)
- ☐ b. say that you must find your own direction (9)
- ☐ c. describe your relationship with an authority figure in your life (4)
- ☐ d. state your feelings about leaders with whom you interact (7)

16. You are talking about relationships; you would probably

- ☐ a. tell about feelings you have for someone close to you (7)
- ☐ b. describe some of your other relationships (4)
- ☐ c. tell what you see happening in this relationship (9)
- ☐ d. express your feelings about leaders with whom you interact (7)

17. You have been talking about the weather; you would probably

- ☐ a. wait for a more interesting topic (1)
- ☐ b. state that this topic seems to come up (6)
- ☐ c. talk about what your family does in this weather (4)
- ☐ d. comment on the behavior of the person you are with (9)

18. The person you are with seems angry at you; you would probably

- ☐ a. remind him/her about the positive aspects of your relationship (8)
- ☐ b. tell what you know about scapegoating (3)
- ☐ c. talk about the increasing tension in all areas of society (3)
- ☐ d. tell how the anger makes you feel (10)

19. You are talking about being close; you would probably

- ☐ a. change the subject (2)
- ☐ b. relate what you and another person have talked about (4)
- ☐ c. talk about a time in the past when you have felt close to the other(s) present (6)
- ☐ d. tell present feeling you are having (10)

20. You are talking about comfort in relationships; you would probably

- ☐ a. suggest an activity (2)
- ☐ b. talk about comfort needs that people feel (3)
- ☐ c. share your feelings about the discussion (10)
- ☐ d. share how you feel when you are with your family (7)

21. You are talking about intimate relationships; you would probably

- ☐ a. talk about limits in relationships (3)
- ☐ b. discuss limits you set in your other relationships (4)
- ☐ c. sit quietly and listen (1)
- ☐ d. tell what you are feeling now (10)

22. Conversation lags; you would probably

- ☐ a. start some "small talk" (2)
- ☐ b. say that you would like to talk (8)
- ☐ c. make an observation on the situation (9)
- ☐ d. ask if the other person is uncomfortable with the situation (8)

23. The other person is angry at you for talking too much; you would probably

- ☐ a. say that he/she seems angry (9)
- ☐ b. relate your feelings about the person's anger (10)
- ☐ c. tell about people you know who talk a great deal (4)
- ☐ d. say that groups always have talkers and non-talkers (3)

24. You are arguing about politics; you would probably

- ☐ a. express your feelings about the conflict (9)
- ☐ b. continue the discussion (3)
- ☐ c. relate how you have felt about similar arguments with others (7)
- ☐ d. describe a discussion you had with (other) friends on the same subject (4)

25. You are involved in intense conflict; you would probably

- ☐ a. talk about how you feel (10)
- ☐ b. talk about conflicts and intimacy in relationships and groups (3)
- ☐ c. state that you are aware of the conflict (9)
- ☐ d. listen to see how the other person(s) feel(s) (1)

26. You have been bored by the conversation for about five minutes; you would probably

- ☐ a. say how you feel (10)
- ☐ b. say you'd like to talk about something else (8)
- ☐ c. tell about your job (4)
- ☐ d. sit quietly and wait for a topic you like (1)

27. The topic is sex; you would probably

- ☐ a. express your feelings toward the other(s) (10)
- ☐ b. tell what you know of sexual behavior (3)
- ☐ c. describe the present interaction (9)
- ☐ d. change the subject (2)

28. You are about to leave; you would probably

- ☐ a. tell what you will be doing later (4)
- ☐ b. recount some important events of the conversation (9)
- ☐ c. tell how you feel about having to leave (10)
- ☐ d. talk about how people say goodbye (3)

29. You are talking about intimacy; you would probably

- ☐ a. tell how you feel about the other(s) (10)
- ☐ b. express what you think you should do to be closer (8)
- ☐ c. tell the person how he/she affects your life (9)
- ☐ d. talk about how you feel about similar situations with others in your life (7)

30. You are trying to evaluate your relationship; you would probably

- ☐ a. talk about various ways to judge a relationship (3)
- ☐ b. ask the other person for a reaction (8)
- ☐ c. express your feelings about the relationship (10)
- ☐ d. recount your observations of this relationship in the past (6).

Now you can compute an Intimacy Orientation score for yourself. *First*, use the response code to determine your score for each item. The response code is the number in parentheses that follows each of the four choices for the 30 items. This number (1-10) indicates an intimacy level for the item response. Circle the response code number for each of the item choices you made. Then add these thirty numbers to determine your intimacy orientation score. Scores range from 85 to 293. The higher your total score, the more intimate your orientation is to the relationship.

Second, think about your score. If it falls below the midpoint (189), you probably prefer what we think of as low intimacy conversation. Do your typical responses focus on the past, outside relationships or impersonal topics? You may be able to see some pattern in your

responses if you examine them carefully. If you do not like your score you may wish to re-examine the response alternatives for each item to get some ideas about behavioral options for your conversational style.

Checking for Intimacy Response Patterns

A number of themes are presented in the items. These themes include feelings, goals, the relationship, authority, intimacy, weather and sex. Use the following procedure with or without a partner:

First, total the number items for which you chose responses coded 8, 9, or 10. These are the most intimate responses.

Next, notice the theme of the responses you chose which are coded 8, 9, or 10. There may be a pattern.

Then examine your responses which were coded 2, 3, and 4. Are there thematic similarities among these items? Now discuss your perceptions of and reactions to your partner's responses with that person.

How Do We Express Control In Our Conversation?

In order to get an idea about how you think you exercise control in conversation, we would like you first to consider the way you interact and talk with people in various situations in your life.

How does a person "control" conversation? To what degree is s(he) directive or responsive? We will use the following instrument, the Control Orientation Technique (COT) to talk and think about the types of control people use as they communicate.

CONTROL ORIENTATION TECHNIQUE

Please rate each of the following items on a scale of 1 to 9, where 1 represents strong *disagreement* and 9 represents strong *agreement*. Do this by placing the appropriate number 1-9 in the space provided at the left of all of the items.

[ ] 1. When having a conversation with a fellow worker I am likely to criticize that person if I feel it's appropriate.

[ ] 2. When I see that a friend has made a mistake I will tell that person exactly what error or mistake he/she is making, and how it can be corrected.

[ ] 3. I often tell persons with whom I am involved in a close relationship what to do.

[ ] 4. If I feel a person I am talking to needs advice I will give it to him/her.

[ ] 5. In a conversation with friends I am likely to express my opinion or supply information when I feel it is appropriate to the topic.

[ ] 6. I am likely to ask questions about my own areas of interest when I am having a conversation with a friend.

[ ] 7. When another person is talking about something that I do not totally understand, I will ask a question to clarify what is being said.

[ ] 8. When another person is expressing strong feelings to me, I listen and accept the feelings by saying something like "I am aware of your strong feelings and can understand them."

[ ] 9. I praise friends and tell them that I appreciate them when they do something I like.

[ ] 10. Sometimes, when in the presence of another person, I remain quiet, not really talking or listening, but "in my own world," or reading, or watching TV.

[ ] 11. If a friend does something I think shows bad judgment, I usually say something like, "you used bad judgment."

[ ] 12. If I see a co-worker making an error, I will tell the person what I think and explain how it could be corrected.

[ ] 13. If I want a person I am with to do something, I am likely to tell that person to do it.

[ ] 14. I freely give advice to other people.

[ ] 15. When talking to another person, I often express my opinion and provide information about the topic under discussion.

[ ] 16. In conversations with friends I think of questions and ask them.

[ ] 17. When I am listening to another person I check my understanding by asking questions.

[ ] 18. I accept or acknowledge statements made by other people in committee work.

[ ] 19. In a relationship, I respond very positively to the other person.

[ ] 20. When I am with a member of my family, I often just sit and think.

[ ] 21. There are times when I criticize or speak sarcastically to another person.

[ ] 22. If a member of my family has problems or makes errors, I will tell that person how to correct the situation.

[ ] 23. I give directions to friends when I feel they need to be told what to do.

[ ] 24. I make suggestions to people if I feel they need to hear my point of view.

[ ] 25. I give my opinion or present facts easily when talking to others.

[ ] 26. In conversation with a fellow worker, I may ask questions based on my own interests.

[ ] 27. If a friend is telling me something, I clarify by questioning her/him.

[ ] 28. When engaged in a conversation I typically listen and acknowledge what I hear.

[ ] 29. It is quite common for me to praise and approve of comments I hear others make.

[ ] 30. When I'm with another person I/we spend the time by sitting silently, not talking to one another.

This series of statements can serve as a basis for thinking about the style of control you exercise in your conversation. You will be able to determine four separate scores. The first is a *Directive To Other* scores. The items in this scale are 1, 2, 3, 4, and 11, 12, 13, 14, and 21, 22, 23, 24. The second is a *Responsive To*

Other scores. This scale includes items 6, 7, 8, 9, and 16, 17, 18, 19, and 26, 27, 28, 29. The third scale is the *Talking* scale and includes items 5, 15, and 25. The last scale, the *Silence* scale is made up of items 10, 20, and 30.

All scores are determined in the same way. For the *Directive* score, total the index values (numbers you chose) for responses to items 1, 2, 3, 4, 11, 12, 13, 14, 21, 22, 23, and 24. This sum is your *Directive* score.

The *Responsive* score can also be determined entering and totaling index values for responses to items 6, 7, 8, 9, 16, 17, 18, 19, 26, 27, 28, and 29. This sum is your *Responsive* score.

The *Talking* score is determined by adding the index numbers for responses to items 5, 15, 25. This sum is your *Talking* Score. The *Silence* score is computed by totaling index values for items 10, 20, 30.

Possible Directive and Responsive scores ranges from 12 to 108. Talking and Silence scores range from 3 to 27.

At this point, you and your partner should each calculate your own scores:

- *a Directive score*
- *a Responsive score*

- *a Talking score*
- *a Silence score*

Now talk over your scores with your partner. Compare your scores and discuss differences. For each of you, which scores are highest, lowest, about the same as your partner's? Give each other feedback.

Remember, no judgments are necessary. You want to check out your perception of your *style.* Are you directive, responsive, quiet? Are you satisfied with your profile? Are you consistent from one situation to another? Check over the items to see if you can gain more insight into the way you may be different in one relationship from another or others, or across different kinds of relationships.

Just How Important Are My Attitudes And Thoughts About Intimacy And Control?

The idea that talking is the way people get started toward intimacy is at some level understood by all of us. We all know that if we are attracted to someone we must talk to each other in order to become intimate. So even if you are a person who feels that "real intimacy" is physical, you know that talking plays an important part in the development of an intimate relationship. For most people a more integrated perception of intimate behavior seems appropriate; we look, listen, talk, and touch in situations where we feel close.

Another way to think about intimacy is how actions make our intimacy goals achievable. Again, let us remember that *there is no one way to improve the intimate relationship, but there are tools and ideas which can be useful to all people* in determining and achieving desired levels of intimacy.

We have presented some paper-and-pencil instruments for assessment of your attitudes toward being close. These may help to clarify some specific feelings about issues closely related to intimacy. Attitudes that seem relevant to most people are highlighted by the following kinds of questions:

- *Do you like to listen to other people talk about themselves?*
- *Do you like to talk about yourself?*
- *Are you concerned about being dominated by others in close relationships?*
- *Are you attracted to most people who are attracted to you?*
- *Do you trust people too much? Too little?*
- *Are you afraid of conflict with people to whom you feel close?*
- *Are you concerned about being rejected by people with whom you have a close relationship?*
- *Are you concerned that close relationships always lead to sex?*
- *Are you reluctant to talk to people about your feelings toward them?*

These questions focus on many of the important attitudes people hold toward intimacy. The central attitudes are those concerned with trust, fear, attraction, rejection, control and privacy.

Most people want intimacy. They may be observed in countless situations trying to move closer to other people. What prevents us from meeting our own intimacy goals? In what ways do our attitudes help or interfere in this quest?

Intimacy is a condition of interpersonal communication that people want. Members of intimate groups feel satisfaction at the times when those groups (couples or larger) feel the very closest to one another. But the road to intimacy is full of blocks. While intimacy is satisfying and exciting, rejection is painful and terrifying. To many people loneliness is preferable to risking rejection or loss of control: "If I get close to another person, then I may have to give up my freedom. I may not be able to do as I please. I will need to consider another person when I make decisions. I may not be able to have my own private life. I may need to curtail the real me."

There is no one attitude that is best for everyone or workable in any relationship at all times. Extreme expressions which reflect desire for intimacy at all costs are at best partly relevant and at worst fraught with serious problems. Statements which emphasize potential risks and losses may indicate attitude patterns that prevent intimacy. Excessive fears related to rejection may prevent people from exploring potentially satisfying relationships. This holds true for those who are constantly concerned about control and have excessive fears of loss of identity as well.

Our discussion of control parallels what we have said about intimacy. Just as people want intimacy, they want to feel powerful and to be seen as having some share of control in a relationship. To explore the parameters of control in a relationship, we seek information primarily through verbal interaction and observation. In these ways we "check out" one another's limits, but we also want to be as aware as possible of our own attitudes toward control in relationships.

When people feel powerless, or are treated as if they were powerless, they may react violently although manipulative responses are more common. Feelings of powerlessness are as painful as loneliness, the lack of intimacy. Feelings of control are possible for all those involved in a relationship. Each person in a relationship influences the "balance of power" or distribution of control in that relationship.

Of course no one really knows what sort of attitude toward control in relationships is "best". The key to all relationships may very well be for both (all) partners to take a positive view toward mutual flexibility. Both people in a relationship contribute to the control of the relationship; ideally, no one feels powerless or "not in control." Both partners in the relationship have a part to play in how the relationship is controlled. It might even be thought of as an expression of "intimate democracy." In this chapter we have attempted to understand our own internal messages about intimacy and control through a consideration of our expectations, symbols, assumptions, beliefs, goals and attitudes. We have also presented some ideas about our orientation to and perceptions of our own behavior. The next step is to start thinking about how we will act in future situations with others. How does the internal message influence ways in which one will act with others?

We are now ready to examine how our talking is related to our own attitudes, assumptions, expectations, and goal messages about intimacy and control. Perhaps you can imagine yourself in a future conversation: How much will I talk? Will I talk about myself? Will I discuss my relationship with the person to whom I am speaking? Will I be open about my feelings? Will I listen? Will I listen to myself? What do I think about what I hear, say and want? Can I learn from my own thoughts so that I get what I want?

CHAPTER 3

Analysis Of Messages In Conversation

Making Messages Work for Us

"I want to get to know you better."

"I am concerned about where this relationship is going."

"I'm involved with my own goals."

"We may be too involved with each other."

These phrases are all from the normal everyday world of talking, but also represent a special type of talking most frequently heard in close relationships.

We are about to present some ideas designed to help increase *awareness of our own conversation,* particularly the talking that we do with those people who are closest to us, to those with whom we share close moments. We assume that:

- *Attention to what we say and how we say it will help us understand the consequences of our statements.*
- *Seeing words as tools in communication will help us to use words with sensitivity to their impact on others.*
- *Understanding our overall pattern of communication will lead us to greater satisfaction and success in our close relations.*
- *Listening to our own statements from the other person's perspective will give us greater control over ourselves.*
- *Reading the message of another person carefully, using all the cues the other sends along with talking, will help us understand what others are thinking, feeling and saying. And finally, by becoming a careful monitor of our own conversations with others, we will significantly improve our opportunities for getting what we want out of our relationships.*

Our approach is to present ideas and methods that can be used to help focus attention on the way we interact, to help us think more specifically about our relations with others.

Understanding our relationships is a key to self knowledge. The tools that are presented in this chapter are designed to help you understand your communication. *They are not evaluation tools.* So as you use the methods presented here, allow yourself to gain greater understanding of your communication style, but be gentle with judgment. Remember, knowledge of yourself and your patterns of talking and relating will help to free you to expand your repertoire of behaviors. Judgment and evaluation may produce anxiety and concern.

The Intimacy and Control Connection

Intimacy and control may be used to describe our behavior. This behavior that we engage in is for many people the *goal of life*: that is, *to feel close and powerful* in important relationships. An important way of looking at our behavior is analysis of our talking.

We assume that the processes of our own interaction are related to our attitudes, goals, perceptions and expectations. By looking at control and intimacy in the actual communication processes, we can gain an understanding of how behavior is related to the direction of conversation and become more skillful in reaching our own goals.

In the last part of this chapter, there is an extensive presentation of categories of intimacy and control. First we wish to explore how they operate in our interaction. Some questions will focus this discussion:

- *Are there expected patterns of control and intimacy expressed in the way we communicate?*
- *Are the patterns related to the type of people, group, and other situational factors?*
- *How are our intimacy and control goals related to these patterns of interaction?*
- *Are there generalizations about patterns of intimacy and control as expressed in language?*

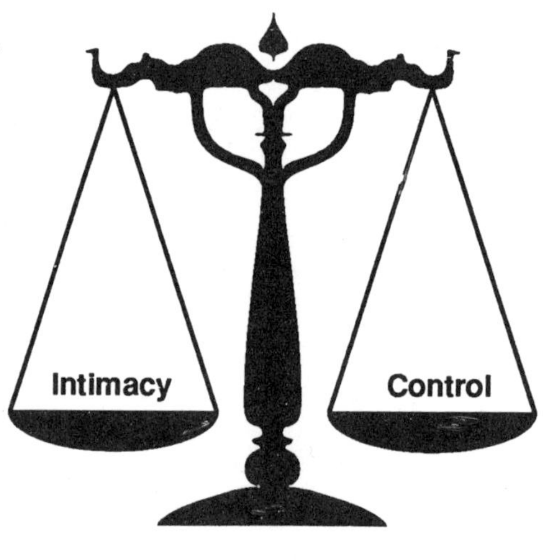

There seem to be general patterns of control and intimacy behavior that we *all* expect, depending on the situation. For example, most of us expect that at a party we might "break the ice" with small talk, but that if we are attracted to someone and become more personal in our talk the reactions from the other person might also become more intimate, and that a pattern toward continued intimacy might develop.

We also might expect that in a work situation with a subordinate, our pattern might at first include providing information, orientation, suggestion and then eventually become directive and corrective. Much depends on our own individual goals and attitudes, but once conversation or interaction has begun, the interaction itself becomes an important cause of what follows. That's why it's so important to be aware of the patterns as they develop.

The development of the intimacy pattern generally moves in the direction of a feeling of closeness over time. In a simple almost self evident sense the more time spent in talking about interpersonal topics, the more likely it is that the talk will either stop or become more intimate. The pattern of intimacy will move from topics of interest significant to the speaker to talk about the speakers' individual lives to talk about one another.

People may talk about their interests, such as sports and music, at some length. Probably individual experience will become part of the conversation at some point. For many relationships, this part of a pattern will be the focus of conversation. In a sense people share their experience with one another. This is an important part of intimacy in most relationships, that is, talking to someone about experiences you have had that the listener has not experienced. For example, when two young people (a boy and a girl) first meet, they may talk at length about school, music they like, and places to go. They also may begin to say things about how their parents treat them, their friends, and their own personal tastes. (Certainly after a date or two they will.) By the time they are "steadies," most of their talk will be about themselves and each other — a lot of it about good and bad feelings they have and wonder about in the other.

Adults who meet at a social gathering will likely talk at first about very general topics and continue to do so with enjoyment even after frequent meetings. Two men will talk about sports, politics, business, maybe religion, women in general, etc. After they have become good friends, they will occasionally speak about the private thoughts and feelings they have about their wives, children, themselves and each other.

If a male "smooth operator" meets an attractive woman at a club, he will probably start talking in an outwardly very intimate manner. It may seem insincere or too forward to the woman, so she may leave or ask him to leave, in words or by her cool manner (the brush off). If not, and if they are attracted to each other, the conversation may begin with the expression of compliments, feelings and desires, but it will probably become less intimate after a while as they back off for a time to get to know each other better. They will talk about their personal lives and experiences, and feelings about others in their lives. After a while, they may move to quite deep levels of personal intimacy, speaking verbally and non-verbally only about each other and feelings.

In all of these situations it appears as though the desire for intimacy is the motivation for the interaction. Perhaps some situations appear to be focused primarily on intimacy and others on control, but of course the apparent focus of nearly all conversation is some mixture. Just as the examples presented here seemed to be concerned with intimacy, we are all aware of situations where the concern appears to be control: Think of the salesman who talks in a ringing, steady "charming" stream of words. Think of the friend who uses big words and abstract ideas, leaving you to admire him in a way, but also to feel excluded and a little disgusted. Recall the person in a meeting who never stops to take a breath so that no one else can get in a word without creating a scene or the ingenuous person who talks about highly interesting or important topics, never stopping. Listeners feel internal pressure not to interrupt. *All these persons are in fact controlling their listeners with their talk,* though one might recognize that the listeners are in a sense agreeing to comply, or the situation couldn't take place.

The Connection Between Intimacy and Control

There appears to be a relationship between intimacy and control, and it's difficult to tell when we want one of the two to the exclusion of the other. So if a person is talking about personal experience, and if the listener is involved at times exchanges his/her own experience, then the focus of control remains flexible.

A clear indicator of verbal control is the amount of talk. If the roles are talker-listener, then talking simply becomes the instrument of control. Telling about one's experience, ideas, or beliefs becomes the controlling agent in conversations.

Generally, the amount of talk becomes controlling particularly when it appears that one person is the talker and the other the listener, and the roles of the participants do not change. Perhaps control becomes an issue in relationships and groups when the balance of participation is such that one person is talking nearly all the time and the other person is not participating verbally. When one of the participants in a conversation does most of the talking, then he/she may also determine the *level* at which the conversation exists. Intimacy and control levels are likely to remain at what might be termed typical, normal, or average in most conversations. By simply exchanging information about experiences that the participants in the conversation have had with others but not with one another, this "average" level of intimacy is maintained.

Under these conditions, control is exerted through talking and the intimacy level is maintained by sharing something that *one* member but not necessarily both feels is significant.

These conditions exist for much of the conversation that we are part of in our daily lives. That is, conversations are not made up of statements that seem to specifically suggest either control or intimacy. The person talking about experiences is referring to those that happened in the past or with people not present. The intimacy message is not stated directly, but rather is suggested indirectly. The same seems true of control. The control message is not sent directly, but rather by focusing the conversation the talker maintains control over the agenda and thus the listener.

Imagine a group of women friends meeting informally over coffee. Can you imagine one of the women enthusiastically talking on and on about her daughter in college? Will the others interrupt her? Probably not, because they are really fond of their friend and want to hear about her daughter. They may feel controlled and held off emotionally, though. In spite of everything, some sort of emotional closeness and feelings of mutual power come about in the group. It happens indirectly, though, and not because the actual word message is focused on these important human conditions which everyone basically desires.

This discussion has focused so far on what might be termed typical conversation. No extreme combinations of intimacy or control have been presented. It seems, however, that the more intimate a conversation becomes, the more likely it is that the level of control will move to one end or the other of the continuum of control.

In terms of our concepts of control and intimacy, if one person begins to talk about her/his relationship with the other, the other person is likely to respond by listening, supporting and clarifying. So an initial attempt at intimacy by one person is followed by less directive control by the other.

Recall the intimacy-control diagram introduced in Chapter 2, and reproduced here. The continuum of intimacy is shown by a horizontal line with words like close and distant used to represent the extremes of this dimension. The vertical line illustrates the control dimension, and the words associated with its extremes are directive and responsive.

The diagram makes it possible to picture the conversation we engage in and to examine how the issues of intimacy and control appear to operate and relate to one another.

EXERCISE

Perhaps one of the most useful tools we can develop is the skill of monitoring our own conversations. A simple exercise may serve to emphasize the point:

Think about the last conversation you had with a person with whom you share a relationship.

1.In which area of the diagram would you locate the conversation?

2.Which area of the diagram shows you the most about your relationship?

3.Is there any part of the diagram that does not seem to apply to your conversation?

4.Think about the various groups in which you hold formal membership. Try to identify the diagram area in which most of group's conversation occurs. Does conversation in most of the groups you participate in seem to be located in one diagram area?

5.Think about your favorite group. If possible, talk with another person who participates in that group. Share the reasons you each like the group. If there is uncertainty, you and the other person can serve as a resource for each other.

6.Share the diagram with your partner and ask him/her to identify the area(s) in which your conversations are located.

In reality, the relationship between intimacy and control is one that constantly changes. At certain times, people may find no issues of control in a relationship. Intimacy has the more important influence. But a change may occur if the relationship appears to be threatened. It may be threatened, in reality, because those in the relationship disagree on how control will be exerted. The question is whether control will be shared or will it be expressed primarily by one person over the other member(s)? As we examine the relationships we have with others, we may find it useful to think about the questions that seem to guide our communication. We assume that there is an important question that we must answer for intimacy and another for control, and that the questions are not separate, but interdependent:

> How close do I want to become to this other person?
> How much control do I want in the relationship?

It seems to be simple in theory.

> "There are certain people with whom I wish to be totally close," and
> "I do not need to be concerned with control in special relationships"

> "Where love and respect exist there is no need for power."

Although these attitudes are widely held, they do not always provide simple answers. The point we emphasize here is that these ideas of intimacy and control are very closely related, do not exist in isolation, and always affect each other.

We do not take these positions independently: control becomes an issue for many as intimacy fails, and intimacy becomes an issue as control fails. Some examples may clarify the point.

If we feel that we have little control in a relationship, (for example, a wife whose husband is "the boss") then we may try to get the more powerful one to become closer.

Also, if a person feels the need to be powerful in relations with others, he/she may try to become intimate or close to people in order to feel more in control with others: "I can influence my friends."

Many people believe that close friends listen, respond, and accept influence from one another. We are all intimate people — that's part of being a person. We are all powerful people also. The question is, what is our relationship or group like?

The difficult problems with intimacy and control may be illustrated by different types of social arrangements. The issues that cause the problems seem to be illustrated by two questions:

- *What is the relation between intimacy and power in our relationship?*
- *What type of relationship does each person want?*

This may mean a constantly changing relationship or it may not. Our concern is *balance.* Balance exists when the expression of control indicates equality among those in the relationship, and expressions of intimacy indicate that conversation among all members is at complementary levels of closeness.

"So is it agreed that we'll save our money and go to the lake next summer instead of the Lodge, Billy?"

"Yeah. I can feel that good water right now!"

"It's fine with me. It means less work for me."

"How about you, Paul?

"I'm happy, Dad, because this way we can all be there."

"Helen, let's go see that new movie at the Ritz tonight. It got great reviews and I really want to see it. The first show is at seven o'clock. You'll love it!"

"Wait a minute. I feel steamrollered. I'd like to see what else there is. Please look at the newspaper, dear. Aw, I know how much you want to see your movie, but please, let's look. I'll get the paper."

People involved with one another do spend much of their time trying to maintain a balance between intimacy and control.

They find that when *conflict* develops it usually has to do with a change in balance between intimacy and control. The imbalance can be expressed in terms of change in perception, attitude or behavior.

"I may change simply because I am letting you see a part of me you didn't see before."

"I kept it from you."

In the early phases of a developing relationship a person exposes himself/herself a little at a time. The initial focus tends to be on intimacy, positive feeling, and harmony. The directive, critical and disapproving parts of a person's behavior are set aside, withheld, minimized or carefully monitored by both partners.

When conflict develops in groups and relationships, it is usually expressed in verbal interaction. One way to start understanding what happens is simply to look at the conversation.

Words are one of our best **tools** for understanding what is happening in our behavior. They are also our *weapons* that we may use to change the nature of a relationship. We give words tremendous power.

Exercise: The War of the Words

Is the word a tool to increase and improve our communication? Many times we have said, "It really got me when you said *blank* in describing me or my behavior."

This exercise has two purposes, first to clarify for each participant those words or phrases that seem to render him/her vulnerable with others and second to sensitize the participant to the area of another person's vulnerability to words.

1. This is done in pairs. Partners individually list ten words that "bother" or are felt to be the most negative. These are the words that they do *not* like used to describe them or their behavior.

2. The lists are then exchanged.

3. Each partner studies the other's list for about five minutes. During this time, try to think about the words and how you feel they fit the person who wrote them. Try to imagine how you would feel if they were said in reference to you. Try to think of something you can say to your partner using some of his/her words to describe your reaction to her/him.

4. Now actually say something to your partner using some of his/her words. Try to say it in a way that you feel will not hurt. Try not to exceed two minutes for this statement.

5. Both members then share reactions to the exercise. Discuss why the word could have hurt. Why didn't it hurt this time? Or if it did hurt, why is the word so powerful?

As we have said, words are used in two ways. They are tools which can be used to communicate and thus form the basis for resolution, new insights, and growth in relationships. Words may alsobe weapons that can be used to "get" the other person, and to establish one person's greater control over other(s) in relationships.

These two statements do not negate the importance of values and attitudes. They simply stress that if we wish to understand our relations with others, we can further our cause by a careful look at our talking. Many ideas are not communicated effectively because the appropriate words are not used.

Some examples will show how we ask for things *indirectly:*

"Uh, would you like to split a coke with me?

"Sure"

"How about splitting it with me now?"

"What do you mean ... oh! You mean go get it. Good grief! "

"I'll get it this time, but no more."

➤➤➤➤

"Say, Bill, you were really brutal to your kid last Saturday when I was here. What was that all about?"

"Well, to tell you the truth I feel terrible about it now. The man next door gave me a lecture on being good neighbors after Davey threw some sand over his fence. I was so embarrassed! I jumped all over poor Dave. He had no idea what was going on, and I haven't explained yet."

➤➤➤➤

If the communication is clarified within the group or relationship, the chances for understanding in the group are increased.

A number of important patterns can be identified by using the diagram introduced on page 98. These seem to be of primary concern to all groups whether they be the couple, family, friendship or a subgroup within some larger organization. Attempts to classify the different types of close relationships that we have is not the same as stereotyping or saying "this is the type I have." Rather it is changeable. Many people have several types of relationships or patterns of relating within one relationship. The first pattern is *sharing* (inclusion, integration, socialization, intimacy, adjustment, communication).

The sharing pattern is characterized by:

- *Fairly intimate (personal, feeling, here and now) communication.*
- *Other reciprocal, empowering controls such as listening are used.*

The levels of intimacy expressed in conversation may not be extreme. People involved in a sharing conversation discuss personal concerns, statements of feelings, reactions to one another. The "sharing" conversation would be located in area C of our diagram. The atmosphere is positive, supportive and intimate.

The sharing pattern may start with "small talk" but will soon shift to personal experiences and feelings that the talkers have with one another. The pattern will eventually be characterized by conversation that is highly personal to both (all) participants.

It is this sharing pattern that many people think of when they refer to:

- *The close relationship they have with their marriage partner.*
- *A new "love" relationship that has developed.*
- *A valued friendship.*
- *The family that they are part of and value.*

The sharing pattern is generally positive, although there may be points of negative feelings. It is also a largely reciprocal pattern. That is, it is not one way communication from one person to other(s), but includes exchanges between members.

A second pattern may be described as *romantic.* This would be located in area A. In this situation the intimacy behavior is close and the control behavior is directive.

The word "romantic" here refers to more "traditional" relationships. Equality is not the targeted control issue. The emphasis is on different roles in the relationship. One person exercises more direction or control than the other(s). This type of situation may also seem to contain a *dependence* of one person on the other: "You are the knight in armor and I'm the beautiful princess."

If the control seems manipulative we need to look at the sequence of interchanges over time. A careful look will show the difference between empowering and manipulation.

The third type of relationship is referred to as *centralized.* This simply means that the control is directive, and the level of intimacy is low. One might describe such a relationship as businesslike, impersonal, informational and intellectual. This is illustrated in area B of the diagram.

A fourth type of relationship may be labeled as *consensual.* This group may be described as participatory, egalitarian, impersonal, factual and agreeable. This is located in area D of the diagram.

All relationships and groups can be located at any specific time in a particular place on this model. One way to view the model is to think of your relationships as being located at different places over time. At first, most "intimate" types of groups like marriages would seem to be in either area A or C. During a fight, a married couple would probably find themselves leaving C and moving to A or B. Serious, prolonged conflict would be indicated by a movement into the extreme part of area A. The conflict may remain in area A as long as the people are expressing the feelings and attitudes toward the relationships they have at that point in time.

Conversation that occurs in area A is often described as painful, frustrating, difficult, damaging, and unnecessary. Frequency, intensity, duration and resolution of conflict detemine its impact on a relationship.

Since the movement of a conversation from area C to area A is often described as a conflict, it is crucial to look at what happens next. Does it keep going deeper and deeper into area A and just stay there? If it does, we would simply call it the *intimate conflict*.

Probably it is not possible for a relationship to remain in area A indefinitely. Rather the discussion is likely to go in one of two ways. First, it may be resolved. Criticism may be clarified by more descriptive language, negative feeling soothed by positive expressions. In this case the conversation would seem to be moving into area C.

This movement is likely when the emphasis on conflict, criticism and control is short in duration. The longer the conflict continues the more likely it is that the conversation would be located in the extremities of area B. Conflict in area B could be described with words such as impersonal, indirect, passive. The fighting could be directed at such things as past behavior of one member, other family members not present, or even at the silence or inattention of one member.

When people engage in what we call non-intimate conflict they often seem involved in an argument that appears to have little if anything to do with them. Such topics as politics, education, sports, religion, entertainment, and philosophy may seem to be the central issues. The discussion may actually move deep into area B, and the conversation may remain there for some time. Area B interactions tend to be characterized by criticism by one and angry silence by the other. Many couples report that this condition of criticism, silence, criticism, silence, silence and more silence may last for days before some change or resolution occurs.

We will look at intimacy first, simply because most people acknowledge intimacy as the reason for forming relationships. The control technique will be presented after we have considered our intimacy style, because power and control seem to have something to do with conflict in relationships, and because control problems appear to be directly related to the destruction of relationships.

Exercise:

In order to begin to think about levels of intimacy in our relationships, let's try an experiment. Think about the situations in which you feel most intimate. You feel close to the other person(s). You feel open and willing to talk and listen. You talk about your feelings directly. You tell the other person(s) about your thoughts, especially those about that person. You especially share your *feelings* about the person. This description suggests what most people think about when they think of intimacy. But you may think about intimacy in different terms. The central point is to think about the "intimate situation." It may contain ideas we are suggesting and it may not.

1. Almost all relationships have some elements of intimacy. We want you to think of the situation in which you feel *most intimate.* After you have thought of one type of intimate relationship or situation, then try to think of another type of relationship.

2. Write down five of these types of relationships. Try to rank them from the most intimate to the least intimate. Before sharing, turn the page and read our list. We want you to do this so that you have an opportunity to check your memory, and make sure you have your list the way you want it. Perhaps you have left something out. This is your chance to check over your list and see if you overlooked anything.

There is no order of intimacy in this list. It includes a variety of interpersonal and group situations that you may want to consider. The list is not exhaustive.

1. Friend of the same sex

2. Co-worker of same sex

3. Marriage partner

4. Family group

5. Attractive stranger in bar, restaurant, waiting room

6. Member(s) of trade organization

7. Attractive stranger on train, plane, bus

8. Casual sexual partner

9. Older friend of family

10. Sibling of the same sex

11. Long standing lover

12. Members of an ongoing group (personal growth, therapy)

13. Member of a women's (or men's) group

14. Members of a committee

15. Members of an organization

16. Co-worker (superior)

17. Co-worker (subordinate)

18. Friend of opposite sex

19. People at a party

20. Neighbor who is an acquaintance

3. When you have written down five relationship types and ranked them, it's time to share them with another person. For this part of the process, there are a number of options:

a) If you are a member of a workshop or class that is using this book, pair up with another member of the group.

b) Your partner could be someone who is a friend, but with whom you do not also have a love or sexual relationship.

c) You could choose a partner for this exercise with whom you share a love or sexual relationship.

d) There is always the option of doing any exercise on your own.

There are many ways to share your lists with one another. Perhaps each of you can simply present your lists to the other, then discuss their likeness and difference. After you have shared your lists with one another, discuss the types of things you would talk about in the most intimate situations. Notice how they are similar to and different from what your partner would discuss.

4. Then discuss those situations that are least intimate. Compare the types of conversations that you have in the less intimate situations with the ones you have in the more intimate relationships.

After you have discussed the differences between intimate conversations, you are ready to go on to study the categories that comprise the Levels of Verbal Intimacy Technique (LOVIT).

How Can We Increase Satisfaction With Our Relationships?

One way to think about our relationships is to consider our conversations and assess our satisfaction with them. Of course we are concerned with the impact important relationships can have on us, and if we don't get what we want from them we may feel unsatisfied.

What should you do to become more intimate so that your relationship will be more satisfying? What *can* you do to accomplish this? Since talking is a main ingredient in your interactions, and probably the only element in your communication that you plan, it may be useful to pay close attention to it and try to determine what is being said in your conversations.

Try this out the next time you feel your conversation with your partner, friend or family member is lacking in the satisfaction you want. Ask yourself:

1. What are my primary feelings?

2. Can I describe what happened?

3. Was any one person more responsible for producing the unsatisfying result?

4. How would my partner answer these questions?

5. How would the conversation have been different if it had been a satisfying experience for me?

What happens if you begin to answer these questions? Do you begin to argue with yourself? Do you find yourself more able to answer all these questions? Do you seem to find it relatively easy to discover what you want to change but are still not able to do it in as complete a way as you would like? Or do you find that you are somewhat confused about what is happening and what you need to do?

Up to this point the focus has been on thinking about what we say to one another, particularly in the context of an important relationship. *It is important to think about our relationships, and view them positively.* We need to see them as sources of influence for ourselves and also as sources for our satisfaction. The need to discover more details about our relationships is the focus of the rest of this chapter. What are the details of our levels and patterns of intimacy and control? Are the intimacy and control patterns clear to us, and how are they related to one another in our own interaction? These questions provide the direction of this chapter.

The Categories for Analysis of Conversation

The concern of this chapter has been the idea that our conversation can be studied by focusing on the two types of behaviors labeled intimacy and control. We will outline and explain specific category systems of behavior that make up the two interpersonal dimensions of intimacy and control: the Levels of Verbal Intimacy Technique (LOVIT) and the Levels of Verbal Control Technique (LOVCT). The LOVIT categories, their descriptions and examples are presented first.

The Levels of Verbal Intimacy Technique (LOVIT)

Most intentional human communication seems to be verbal. How can we develop an understanding of what happens when people talk (communicate verbally)? Systematic observation of talking in small groups can help us understand what people are doing and how as members and leaders we can gain more insight into our own relationships with others. Systematic awareness of our own behavior is fundamentally valuable in making decisions about how we will behave.

The focus of this section is on the development of intimacy behavior in a group. One way to approach the problem is to classify the things people say and do with each other along a continuum from least intimate to most intimate. Ten categories or *levels of behavior* in a group are scaled from least intimate to most intimate. The purpose of this section is to present and describe the ten levels, and then provide examples for each category. The intimacy continuum extends from level one (least intimate) to level ten (most intimate).

Level 1: Silence, no single conversation

This first level is used to describe a group when members are carrying on more than one conversation simultaneously. The situation is affected somewhat by group size. In smaller groups of two to five persons we are somewhat less likely to find several conversations at the same time. Included in level one is the situation when *no* member of the group is talking.

This level of verbal intimacy is used when there is *no single* discussion going on within the group. The group does not look or sound like a group. Members sit in *silence,* or in smaller groups. People may be sitting passively with little movement, often looking away from others.

Another type of behavior at this level is *noise.* Noise occurs when two or more members are talking at the same time. This includes periods when people interrupt each other, or when one member starts to talk while another member is still talking and the interrupted member continues to talk.

Two or more simultaneous conversations presents another example of Category One. This may be observed in what appears to be a single group formation, one person is interacting with a part of the group. If there are only two people in the group, this category is applied somewhat differently. In the case of a couple or other two person group, both members may be in the same place at the same time, but they are not talking to one another. Examples of this occur throughout the lives of most married couples; one of the members of a couple may be talking while the other is reading or watching TV. A common experience in a marriage relationship is for the two partners to be together in the same place and yet for both to have their thoughts focused somewhere other than the relationship or the other person.

A summary of the various types of behavior classified at *level one* includes the following:

- ☐ Two or more separate conversations are going on in the group at the same time.
- ☐ One private conversation in the presence of silence in the rest of the group when the private conversation is not directed to the rest of the group.
- ☐ Silence in the group that lasts for 10 seconds or longer.
- ☐ Two or more members talking at once for 10 or-more seconds.
- ☐ Noise such as laughter, singing, yelling, screaming, etc., that lasts for at least 10 seconds.
- ☐ Members of a group of two are not talking to each other (reading, watching TV or perhaps one person talking on the phone).
- ☐ Indeterminable statements that can't be classified because they can't be heard well enough.
- ☐ Indeterminable statements that do not seem to belong in any of the other nine categories.

Some examples will illustrate the level of verbal intimacy that is likely to exist when the group is doing those things that we call level one activity. Level One behavior is not verbally intimate. Of course nonverbal intimacy can exist even when there is no talking. Consider the following examples.

- ☐ Two people having a romantic dinner, no talking but hand holding and eye contact. Perhaps some kissing. No intimacy in words, but in feeling there is intimacy.
- ☐ A quiet family evening around the fire, after dinner and dishes are done.
- ☐ A class that is all talking in small bunches of 2 or 3 in lowered tones, before the teacher comes in.
- ☐ A class that is talking and laughing loudly, just before recess.
- ☐ Four people in a car, riding silently, lost in their thoughts.
- ☐ Some people in a restaurant whose conversation we can't hear because of noise from the kitchen.
- ☐ Kids playing and just making funny noises.
- ☐ A group of people singing around the piano.

Level 2: Small Talk, verbal exchange

Level 2 includes many of the kinds of things that people talk about when they don't know each other very well. Basically, this level includes those things that people talk about when they are *not talking about their own present or past experience.*

In some ways this category contains statements that do not clearly fit into any of the other categories. Statements concerned with people and their relationships in general, statements about the group and about those experiences members have had outside the group are *not included* at this level. Even with the above restrictions, there are many examples of statements in this category in all of our daily conversations.

Those statements that we often think of as small talk, or cocktail-party talk are included in this lowest level of verbal intimacy. Level 2 statements are about topics that concern us but over which we have little or no control, and no involvement except perhaps as observers. We are all aware of the weather and it effects, but we don't participate in it except as observers, victims or beneficiaries.

A conversation at this level of intimacy could include any one of a large number of topics or issues that people talk about when they are at meetings, informal gatherings or in work relationships. Some examples of these topics are the academic disciplines, sciences, language,art, music, automobiles, houses, yards, nature, sports, and important people. Specific discussions about individuals not known by members of the group, like political figures or famous people, fall in this category. Discussion about much of what appears in the newspapers would be included in Level 2.

Expressions of feelings, values and attitudes are included in this category if the value, feeling or attitude is expressed toward someone or something that is not part of a member's experience. Examples would be feelings about or attitudes toward the President, war, the United Nations, or movies. Also included are statements of feelings or attitudes toward things in a person's life such as food or the weather.

"I can't stand broccoli."

"I really love this warm weather."

Another type of Level 2 statements includes routine or perfunctory statements like, "How was your weekend?" or "How do you feel?" Many of these statements may lead into more intimate categories, but they do start in Category Two. An example of this might be, "How are you?" followed by, "I am terrible. I had an awful fight with my wife." At this point, the discussion would have moved to Level 7.

The following examples may clarify the types of statements that are included in Level 2:

- ☐ Nice weather we're having.
- ☐ The baseball season is too long.
- ☐ The medical profession is just another political organization.
- ☐ Machines do more and more work for people.
- ☐ Most big cities have a pollution problem.
- ☐ School busing is a hot potato.
- ☐ The Viet Nam war was a mistake, but then so were all the wars.

- ☐ The existence of green trees is necessary for life; it's an example of how important all life is to our life.
- ☐ I love the music of the great masters.
- ☐ I have a very large front yard.
- ☐ I live in a practically new house.
- ☐ My car uses too much gasoline.
- ☐ About 50 percent or more of the people in the U.S. cannot identify their ethnic origins. And fifty percent of those who do are mistaken.
- ☐ Money may not be necessary, but it's good to have.
- ☐ I think that movies are getting too sex-oriented.
- ☐ We are all in it — that is life!

How much of the talking in your life is at this level? Do you like it the way it is? How much time you spend talking at this level with those with whom you are most intimate? Perhaps you are not sure. Maybe you need to observe "the two of you." Now it will be possible for you to notice how much small talk there is in your closest relationships. Remember that much of the small talk we engage in within our most intimate relationships we look upon as fun. Small talk is not bad. The issue for each of us is how we feel about *amount* of small talk we engage in.

Play a little game with yourself. Think of five "memorable" conversations you have had with five different people or groups of people during the last week. Now rank the five conversations from most small talk to least small talk. Are you surprised at the ranking? Do you wish that any of the conversations were less small talk and more personal talk? Think about how you might change the conversation.

Level 3: People in General

This category includes discussions about people and their relationships. Such topics as leadership, membership, conflict in groups and issues of interpersonal relations also are located in this category. Included are discussions about the nature and function of different kinds of groups such as committees, therapy, encounter, sensitivity, men's, women's, professional, business, educational and family groups. The main guideline to follow in using this category is that *statements refer to groups or relationships among people in general and do not refer to specific people or relationships among specific people.* If a statement refers to ideas about groups or interpersonal relations in general, it probably belongs in this category. If it refers to a *specific group or interpersonal situation that the speaker has experienced, then it belongs in another category.* Conversations about two person groups like marriages or parent-child relationships, or the behavior of a person within one of those types of relationships, are also included in Level 3. Some examples would be:

- ☐ It's healthier if husbands and wives don't tell each other everything.
- ☐ Some people invite conflict in order to avoid more intimate relationships.
- ☐ Children tend to resist parental authority.

A second type of statement includes *descriptions of groups in general:*

- ☐ Groups need goals.
- ☐ The definition of a group is two or more people interacting with each other.
- ☐ The more time they spend together, the closer people become.

Another type of statement that falls in Level 3 is the *discussion of different types of groups:*

- ☐ There are three types of groups: work groups, social groups and educational groups.
- ☐ We see more types of groups all the time.

Much discussion of groups centers on the *description of various theories of group behavior.* Some examples would be:

- ☐ Groups move through various phases, according to Schutz.
- ☐ The sociometric approach can help members understand groups.

Another type of statement included in Level 3 is concerned with the *psychology of groups.* When the speaker is talking about ideas and concepts of social psychology, Level 3 is probably the appropriate category:

- ☐ Rejection is caused by competition.

- ☐ Norms develop through interaction.
- ☐ Leadership is a group function.

The last type of statement in category three includes those statements that express *feelings, beliefs, attitudes or values that members have about groups in general:*

- ☐ Groups do not really do any good.
- ☐ I feel that groups are very destructive.
- ☐ The only good group is a dead group.
- ☐ Groups are really good for people.

Some additional examples include:

- ☐ People waiting for a bus together don't usually talk to each other.
- ☐ People in a critical situation often form a group very rapidly.
- ☐ Groups must have goals, structure and leadership in order to function.

Levels 2 and 3 are impersonal and distant from here and now experience. Statements refer to things and people removed from the present group by distance, whether the distance is psychological or physical.

Although Levels 2 and 3 represent a relatively low level of intimacy, the total pattern of conversation will clarify the role that talk in these levels plays in the development of intimacy in a conversation.

We are going to refer to this type of conversation as "people in general." But it is in fact a type of *small talk about people in general,* as well as one way of talking about oneself in an indirect or disguised manner:

- ☐ If you don't stay on your guard in life people will take advantage of you. People need to protect themselves and their family. No one else is going to do it.
- ☐ You really think that?
- ☐ People will take what they can get — only the strong have a chance.

Because intimacy is a concept that has little meaning except as applied to people, this small talk about people in general appears more intimate than the other small talk referred to in Level 2.

Level 4: Outside the group: Individual experience

The talking classified in Level 4 is *personal to the speaker.* It is psychologically close to the speaker, but may not be close to the listener. It does have an effect on the listener(s) that may help the listener feel close to the speaker.

"If the speaker sounds like the kind of person I can trust, then I will probably want to say something about myself."

Level 4 statements are more intimate than Level 3 statements because of personal involvement of one member with the topic of conversation. *The more people are involved in the content of a discussion, the more involved they will become with the members of a group.*

The first thing many people think about telling others is something about their life and experience outside the present group. Any time a person is talking about personal experiences rather than expressing feelings about his or her life, this category is used. The category includes personal background information and facts about what has happened to a person. Examples of these types of statements are:

- ☐ I grew up in a small town in the middle west.
- ☐ I moved so much when I was a child that I attended over 20 different schools.
- ☐ My older brother and I did everything together until I graduated from college.
- ☐ Last summer we went to Canada.
- ☐ My father was a construction worker.
- ☐ Both my stepfather and mother have been divorced.
- ☐ I'm half French and half Irish.
- ☐ For ten years our family has gone camping in the Poconos every June.
- ☐ In 1970 I got my doctorate.

☐ I'm the youngest in my family.

A second type of discussion included in this category is talk about *present experiences outside the group,* or *information about the present life of the speaker.* Facts about the personal life, job, or other activities that the speaker is involved in are included.

Some examples are:

☐ This program I am enrolled in requires that I attend 3 meetings a month on Monday nights.

☐ I have been a member of a political group for over three years now.

☐ I haven't gotten much sleep this week.

☐ I'm in the pizza business.

☐ My job requires that I travel a lot.

☐ I'm married with three kids.

☐ I live in Oak Park.

☐ I'm a C.P.A.

☐ Activities at the Temple take up a lot of my time.

☐ My wife's folks are with us.

☐ My kids are going through chicken pox.

A third type of statement in this category involves *talking about the future.* Statements of intention, proposals, or plans could be included. Examples include:

- ☐ I am going to move to California someday.
- ☐ In the fall, I will go back to school.
- ☐ The job situation is such that I will change jobs next year.
- ☐ I am going to try to spend more time in physical activity next year.
- ☐ This summer I will go swimming every day.
- ☐ I am going to vote for a winner in the presidential election this fall.
- ☐ In ten years I'll have a new body.
- ☐ I'll stop smoking on my birthday.
- ☐ This is the last time I'll pledge to that charity.
- ☐ Someday I'll go back to school and finish my degree.
- ☐ When I retire I'll open a small printing-publishing shop.

Some of the most difficult statements to classify are those which appear to have a strong emotional component associated with deep *self-disclosure*. Such statements are classified in Level 4 unless the tone of voice or other nonverbal cues indicate they should be classified in Level 7. An example would be, "I have been in prison." As it stands it seems to be classified in Level 4, but if stated with emotional overtones or the context clearly indicates an expression of emotion, the statement would belong in Level 7.

Other examples of Level 4 include:

- ☐ I am a carpenter.
- ☐ I have been a member of the Catholic church all my life.
- ☐ Someday soon I'm going to take a course in Yoga.
- ☐ People come up to me on the street and tell me things that they wouldn't normally tell close friends.
- ☐ A teacher of mine asks questions and then waits 3 or 4 minutes to see if there is an answer.
- ☐ Any play I was ever in as a kid — I was always a rabbit.
- ☐ I voted for Carter, Kennedy, and Goldwater.
- ☐ One thing about me is, I never let a friend down.
- ☐ I've made a lot of mistakes in my life.
- ☐ After my first wife died, I moved to Cincinnati.
- ☐ This suit was on sale at Golden Harry's...
- ☐ At one time I thought of being a night club singer.

Level 5: Outside the Group: Shared Experience

Level 5 is more intimate than Level 4 because *those things being talked about are personal experiences for more than just one member of the group.* The personal experience "shared by part of the group" may also be of interest to other group members because of the fact that when a subgroup from a larger group meets, its topic of conversation often becomes "the rest of the group." Level 5 includes all statements regarding subgroups of the membership that have gotten together outside the group. It also includes statements about future activities group members will share outside of the group. Statements of this nature do not require the outside activity to be group related. This category may provide information about subgroups that exist outside of the group. Information of this nature may be helpful in determining the structure of subgroups operating within the group as well. Level 5 is considered mid-range on the intimacy scale because it represents statements that have some group centered content. However, this content may be minimal, given that discussion probably does not refer to the group as a whole, is not in reference to the present situation, and is not necessarily directly associated with feelings.

Some examples of Level 5 statements are listed below. These will give you a more complete understanding of the verbal statements that should be classified in Level 5:

- ☐ Harry, Jean and I stopped for a drink after our group session last week.
- ☐ I asked Sarah to spend the afternoon with me.
- ☐ Jack and I are planning to go to a game together this Sunday.
- ☐ Mary and I talk about the group almost every day over lunch.
- ☐ You know, one of these days Sam and I will get together over coffee and settle this thing.

☐ During the break four of us came up with this great idea! You should hear what he and I say about the rest of you when we're driving home afterwards!

☐ If there's more talk like that, Henry and Thelma and I will probably go off and form our own group.

Statements of this nature differ from Level 4 (description or narrative of events in a member's life) in one major way. Category 5 "talk" always includes at least one person other than the speaker who is a member of the current group. It also includes statements made about the activities of two or more group members who knew each other before the group's life began. For example, group members Mary and Sue have known each other for three years. In a group meeting Sue says, "Mary and I had a rough time with the administration where we worked last year." This statement is a description of events in a member's life, but the events involved two members of the present group.

Another type of statement classified in Level 5 is conversation about one or more group members who are not present. Examples of this abound in our everyday experience. Two parents talk about one of their children. Two friends meet and talk about a third mutual friend. Persons in a group discuss a missing member or members.

In these conversations the focus is on only a part of the group. The talk is usually focused on the past or future rather than on the here and now. Examples would be:

- ☐ I feel that Jerry is improving in the way he relates to me. *(Jerry is not present)*
- ☐ I wonder where John is?
- ☐ Now that she's gone, please tell me what you heard about her.
- ☐ Pay attention now, we have only 15 minutes to do this before he comes back.
- ☐ I know it's not nice to talk about someone who's not here, but I'll never understand that boy.

A final issue pertinent to this category concerns the operational definition of subgroup. The definition of Level 5 states "... experiences which *two or more* group members..." At what point does a subgroup take on the properties of the whole group? For the purpose of classification, statements made about an activity outside of the group which involve *less than one-half* of the entire group are Level 5 statements. If more than one-half of the group membership is involved, the statement would then be considered for classification in Level 6.

Level 6: Group Experience: Past, Future, Hypothetical

The focus of this category is the present group. The statements included are: (a) about the past, (b) the future, and (c) general statements about the present group.

One of the most important topics groups discuss is their immediate past experience. *For this category system the past is defined as anything that occurred before the beginning of the present meeting.* Therefore, when people are discussing things that happened at a previous group meeting held earlier in the same day or the day before, such talk would be classified in this category. Some examples would be:

- ☐ Last week we had a meeting with lots of silence.
- ☐ Alice used to get annoyed when we pushed to get closer.
- ☐ The last time you and I talked about this, I was confused.
- ☐ We had a lot of conflict last week.
- ☐ The group had no goals this morning.
- ☐ It was really hard for everyone last week.
- ☐ The last time we met has got to be the worst meeting we ever had.
- ☐ We're still feeling good about our time together.
- ☐ I wish I could forget what happened yesterday. I acted like an idiot.

Statements about the *present group* that are not clearly related to the *present meeting* are included in Level 6. Such statements could be considered generalizations about the present group, but are not clearly descriptions of the current meeting:

- ☐ Our group is a fun loving group.
- ☐ We have our ups and downs.
- ☐ This group has always been in flight.
- ☐ This is a group that works very hard.
- ☐ The group seems to have difficulty getting started at every session.
- ☐ This is the way we always are together.
- ☐ It seems that whenever anyone makes a generalization about the goal, the members stop talking.
- ☐ As couples go, we're average, I suppose.
- ☐ Our family is close-knit.
- ☐ This team has spirit.

References to the *future of the group* also fall into this category. This kind of statement centers around the expectations held by group members or those in a relationship about what the group or relationship will be like in the future. Also included are statements that do not include a time reference, as well as predictions, fantasies, and hypotheses. Much of the discussion among members about the group is Level 6 talk because this is a way members can become involved in whole group discussion and still maintain an orientation to their experience that is somewhat distant, detached, objective, and comfortable. Some examples of the kind of statement just described would be:

- ☐ This group is eventually going to need a goal.
- ☐ There is always going to be conflict in the group.
- ☐ I think we can expect to have discussions like this as long as we know each other.
- ☐ From the beginning — and I assume as long as we are a group — we seem to be saying the same thing over and over.
- ☐ Since we first met I think we've come to know each other very fast.
- ☐ We'll always love each other.
- ☐ Yes, there'll be a lot of changes taking place among us.
- ☐ No organization ever gets by "scot free!"
- ☐ Like any other group, we'll have our ups and downs.
- ☐ Oh, I wish we could get along better.

Level 7: Outside the group: Feelings About Individual Experience

This category includes expressions of a group member's feelings about events in her/his life outside of the group. Usually, statements of this nature will be made in the first person. Examples:

- ☐ My husband is really frustrating me these days.
- ☐ The kids had me so tense last night that I found it almost impossible to sleep.
- ☐ I have recurring nightmares that terrify me.
- ☐ Last spring I took the best class of my life!
- ☐ My family moved to Iowa when I was 15 and I've never gotten over having to leave my old friends.
- ☐ New York was so exciting last week.
- ☐ I've got a new boyfriend and I'm thrilled!
- ☐ At last all my children are out of college.
- ☐ At the dentist's Monday, it hurt so bad I cried.

Another member of the group may seek to clarify material in this category. Attempts may also be made to probe more deeply into the incident and its effects. Such actions by other members often are in the form of questions, open ended statements, or empathic remarks. *Any verbal interaction that serves to keep the group focus on the incident* is classified in Level 7. Examples:

- ☐ How are you attempting to deal with the frustration caused by your husband?
- ☐ Sleepless nights are no fun.
- ☐ I can see how a scary dream would be upsetting.
- ☐ What did you like about that class that was so great?
- ☐ You really missed your school pals when you moved.

- ☐ New York is always exciting for me, too.
- ☐ Who is this new dreamboat you met?
- ☐ Think of the money you can save now that your kids are out of school!

Only statements *expressing emotion about incidents not related to the group* are included in Level 7. Discussions in Level 7 often progress to a higher numbered, more intimate category. For example, other members may respond to a person's description of an incident in the following ways:

- ☐ You seem to have brought that frustration into the group with you today.
- ☐ It looks like the tension caused by your kids is still with you.
- ☐ Are you upset now that we are talking about your nightmares?
- ☐ How was that spring class better than this one?
- ☐ Do you think the past affects your attitude toward us?
- ☐ Well, New York is great, but what's that got to do with us right now?
- ☐ You should see the glow of love on your face!

These statements and questions clearly relate Level 7 discussion to the context of the present group. Based on the content, the interaction may move to either Levels 8, 9, or 10. The focal person may also take the discussion to another category:

- ☐ How was that spring class better than this one? (Possibly moves the discussion into Level 8)
- ☐ Do you think the past affects your attitude toward us? (Possibly moves the conversation into Level 8).
- ☐ Well, New York is great, but what's that got to do with us right now? (Possibly moves the discussion into Level 9).
- ☐ You should see the glow of love on your face! (Seems to move the discussion into Level 9).

Level 8: Inside the group: Indirect Expression of Feeling

Level 8 talk includes expression of feeling that is indirectly stated, does not clearly say that the feeling is the speaker's, and does not include clear labeling or naming of the feeling. Feeling is said to be expressed indirectly when the criteria of ownership of feeling and labeling the feeling are not met. The most frequently used ways to express feelings indirectly are through the expression of value, opinion, question, reference and tone of voice. *Levels and statements that place values* on the group, people in the group, or things that have been said in the group. These are most often made with reference to whether a thing is good or bad, or appropriate or inappropriate. Another way to think about these statements is that they are related to standards that members of the group have or have not met. These statements usually include words like good, right, appropriate, wrong, bad, mistake, and sometimes "I can't agree with you."

Words like *ought* and *should* can also signal the use of this category. Some examples of Level 8 statements are:

- ☐ This is a really terrific group.
- ☐ We shouldn't have done it that way.
- ☐ We really ought to try it and I think it will be better than what we did.
- ☐ You made a mistake in the way you expressed that feeling.
- ☐ The way you handled that did a lot of good for the group.
- ☐ Try that again, get some feedback, and you will do a better job.
- ☐ You can't do that, it's not good for the group.
- ☐ Wait a minute, we just can't do things this way.
- ☐ This is all wrong.
- ☐ Beautiful! Beautiful!

A second type of statement that falls into this category involves explaining one's behavior or apologizing. When members explain to the group or a person in the group why they did something, the statement is placed in Level 8. The following examples illustrate these kinds of statements:

- ☐ I didn't mean to say what I did.
- ☐ I couldn't help it.
- ☐ I did it because I felt it would help clarify and explain why I did it.
- ☐ Well now, just wait a minute! I can explain.
- ☐ Now let's be reasonable. I did that because you pushed me.
- ☐ I couldn't resist saying this.
- ☐ I'm just the mouthpiece for the group.
- ☐ Now wait a minute. I'm not the only one who feels this way.

Another behavior that indicates indirect expression of feeling is a statement that communicates denial of feeling. This category does not imply the existence of a feeling in all cases, but the act of denial does indicate that the speaker probably has some feeling (discomfort, resistance) about being labeled as having the feelings. Classification in this category is much clearer when the verbal behavior is supported by some nonverbal indicator. Therefore, the statement needs to be made in such a way that the tone of voice or some other quality of the voice makes it clear that the person is expressing a feeling. Examples would be:

- ☐ I don't care — I don't have any feelings.
- ☐ That did not make me the least bit angry.
- ☐ It never bothers me when people criticize me.

- ☐ I don't know why you think it bothers me. I don't feel attacked.
- ☐ I don't feel defensive - I don't even care what you say about me.
- ☐ To hell with it.
- ☐ I quit. I don't care any more.
- ☐ I wash my hands of the whole thing.

Emotion is often expressed indirectly through the use of questions. In this way the speaker may invite another member to express the feelings directly. Examples would be:

- ☐ How do you feel about that?
- ☐ How angry do you feel about what's happening?
- ☐ Are you upset about what I said?
- ☐ Do you feel good now?

Another method of expressing feelings and emotions indirectly is through a *reference* to another or others. The feeling is indirect because the criterion of *ownership of the feeling* is not met: the person allows others to represent his/her feelings. When a person expresses feelings in this way it is not clear that the feeling really belongs to the speaker. The speaker makes ownership of the feeling unclear through the use of an indefinite or uncertain reference to the owner of the feeling. Some examples of this type of statement are:

- ☐ People get really angry over that kind of thing.
- ☐ We really enjoy this type of discussion.
- ☐ Well, let's hear how you really feel.
- ☐ Don't tell me that the group is just going to sit there after what happened!
- ☐ Come on now, what's really going on with all of you?
- ☐ That is the kind of thing that can really depress the members of this group.
- ☐ We're glad you're back in the group.
- ☐ One feels sad when one sees the conflicts.
- ☐ Anyone would feel bad if that happened to them.
- ☐ We feel very angry with you now.
- ☐ Most of the members are very angry.
- ☐ I think we are very uncomfortable about that.
- ☐ The group is quite satisfied.
- ☐ We all feel bad about that.

What do you see in yourself? Think about the most positive messages you have sent verbally in the last week. Think about three of the most positive and then contrast those with the three most negative. Were they said the way you wanted? How indirect are you? How about the person in your closest relationship? Does he/she use many indirect statements? Are you compatible? Are you both indirect in expressing feeling? Are you direct? Are your styles mixed?

Level 9: Inside the Group: Description of Experience

All statements describing the "here and now" experience of the group are placed in this category. These types of verbal interaction can be broken down into more specific behaviors. Here and now experiences are defined as events happening at the moment as well as anything which occurred during the present meeting. Descriptive statements are used when people want to talk about their shared experiences. It also includes the following types of statements:

a) Statements that attempt to clarify or restate a statement made by another person, for example, "I hear you saying that the group is working on its problem."

b) Statements that are group oriented and deal with events and activities which are occurring or have occurred in the present meeting. Conversation of this type is often used to analyze feelings or attitudes that are present in a relationship.

Some examples of Level 9 are:

- ☐ It seems to me the group is very quiet today.
- ☐ I'm feeling a lot more comfortable with myself today.
- ☐ Every comment you made after that, you referred back to him.
- ☐ I was going to ask Jeff if he would give us some direction.

- ☐ The group doesn't have a task orientation now, but what do we do when the group moves in that direction and someone doesn't choose to go along?
- ☐ People (referring to group) are very stiff about being observed.
- ☐ But I don't understand why it annoys you.
- ☐ I'm starting to think this is a structured unstructured group, and it's very unclear.
- ☐ I think that Charlie drew a parallel.
- ☐ How does it relate to me, to us, the group?
- ☐ I asked you to join the group but you are still quiet.
- ☐ I would like to say a couple of potentially analytical things about their roles and what happened today.
- ☐ What is everybody else thinking?
- ☐ It's unusual for me to be quiet in a group, as I am today.
- ☐ You sound like you have a need for direction.
- ☐ I haven't gotten quite that reading.
- ☐ I need smiles right now
- ☐ Why are you concerned about silence?
- ☐ I was thinking about silence in terms of the silence in the group now.
- ☐ Now, let's analyze it.

c) Self descriptions that are stated in the present, or those that contrast the speaker's present self with the past are behaviors that would be classified in this category:

"I am a very careful person in this group. I think carefully and choose my words carefully. I thought for five minutes before I said that."

"You did?"

"Yes, and I am now weighing all my words."

How much of what you observe and think do you verbalize? Do you share as much as you want? Most of us have a tendency *not to* share our thoughts and perceptions. Why do you think it's that way?

Level 10: Inside the Group: Direct Expression of Feeling

The ideas that seem most central to intimacy may be best illustrated by behavior in this category. Earlier, we suggested that the most intimate types of conversation are focused inside a group or relationship. When people are speaking *to* those they are talking about, and when they are expressing their feelings directly, then their conversation is at the highest level of intimacy.

This category at the extreme of the continuum includes those statements that are *most intimate.* The criteria that must be met therefore include the here and now criteria met for the previous category, but also include others. Specifically the criteria for Level 10 are (1) Direct statement to the person or group, (2) *Here and now* expression of feeling, (3) Clear ownership of the feeling by speaker, and (4) The use of a *feeling related word*. Some examples are:

- ☐ I am angry at the group right now because it just ignored my comment.
- ☐ I like you very much because of something you are doing during this meeting.
- ☐ I'm so happy now!
- ☐ Don't speak to me for a while. I'm depressed.
- ☐ You know, I never quite felt this way before.
- ☐ Wait, I feel like you're pushing me. Suppose we start over again. What is it you want of me?
- ☐ I feel so calm now. The group has reached a new level, and I'm feeling great.
- ☐ Even though the group is fighting, I feel clear and centered.

These comments are clearly stated in the here and now. Reference is made to the present. They also meet the criterion of ownership because the speaker is saying that "*I* have the feelings" and making it clear that "I am the angry one" in the first example and in the second example it is the person speaking who likes the other person. The third criterion, making it clear that the *speaker has a feeling,* is also met through the use of a feeling word, either "like" or "angry."

For the purpose of this category system, "feeling words" are defined rather narrowly. The typical list of emotions includes (among others) fear, anger, joy, and excitement. To illustrate this point, a list of the most frequently occurring words that indicate feelings will be presented in the next section. Whenever one of these words is used in a context that meets the other criteria, the use of Level 10 is appropriate. Often the word "feel" is followed by a *belief statement* in conversation. For example: "I feel that you are making a mistake." "How do you feel you did on that test?" "This country feels like it's time for a change!" "I'm afraid I don't feel good about what you just did." "I don't know how the committee is going to feel about giving just 'pass' or 'fail' in a course."

Another type of statement that falls in Level 10 is a statement that appears by use of a modifying word or phrase not to meet the criteria. Some examples are:

- ☐ I am getting angry.
- ☐ I think I am frustrated with you.
- ☐ I may be angry with you.
- ☐ Maybe I am angry with you.
- ☐ I suppose I am really frustrated.
- ☐ If this keeps up I'll be the happiest man alive.
- ☐ It's possible that I'm depressed.
- ☐ When you act like that, I feel shocked.

Because of the importance and complexity of this category, a number of additional examples are presented here:

- ☐ I feel very angry with the whole group right now.
- ☐ I'm really happy to be here right now.
- ☐ I am attracted to you.
- ☐ My reaction to that exercise you suggested is fear.
- ☐ I feel rejected by the group.
- ☐ I feel good about what you said to me.
- ☐ I feel so bad, I wish I'd never come tonight.
- ☐ When I walked in the room I felt tense, and I still feel tense.
- ☐ I feel so warm and relaxed — nothing could bother me.
- ☐ I'm getting angry — I'm getting angry!
- ☐ When you smile at me like that, I feel all sorted out and connected inside.
- ☐ I feel like jumping for joy!
- ☐ Uh-oh, I feel myself getting tight and defensive now.

Words That Indicate Feelings

Some of the most frequently used feeling words are presented on the next two pages in order to aid identification of the feeling as it is used in this category (Level 10). Words most often associated with positive feelings are listed on page 153, and words normally associated with negative feelings are listed on page 154.

There is another way that the feeling-word criterion can be met, and that is by using another word in combination with the word "feeling." Phrases like "feel good," "feel wonderful," "feel terrific," "feel bad" are all examples of a pair of words that label the feeling a person is expressing. In most uses these words express value judgments, but when combined with "I feel" indicate a direct expression of feeling.

Another kind of feeling that is classified in this category includes several types of statements that do not appear to meet the criteria. Some of these are *feelings expressed in the past tense but said in reaction to something that happened in the present group session.* An example would be, "I felt bad when you said at the beginning of the session that you didn't trust me." As long as the feelings are in the here and now or *occurred in the present session,* they can be classified in this category.

The categories for Levels of Verbal Intimacy Technique (LOVIT) have been designed for use in training and self understanding. This method can be

POSITIVE FEELING WORDS

love
adore
idolize
want

infatuated
tender
vibrant
capable

delighted
eager
optimistic
joyful
hopeful

strong
gay
good
inspired

pleased
euphoria
moved
placid
alert

jolly
relieved
glad
venturous
peaceful

attractive
turned on
worthy

respect
empathy
awed
happy
great
proud
gratified
admire

strong
amused
secure
popular

valiant
brave
brilliant
liked
cared for

friendly
regarded
benevolent
wide awake
at ease

appreciate
warm
graceful
amused

elation
enthusiastic
zealous
courageous
enchanted
sympathetic
important

esteemed
affectionate
fond
excited
patient

exhilarated
attracted
peaceful
satisfied
sensitive

appreciated
consoled
peaceful
appealing

relaxed
comfortable
content
keen
amused
pleased

exotic
high
alive
tranquil
sure

NEGATIVE FEELING WORDS

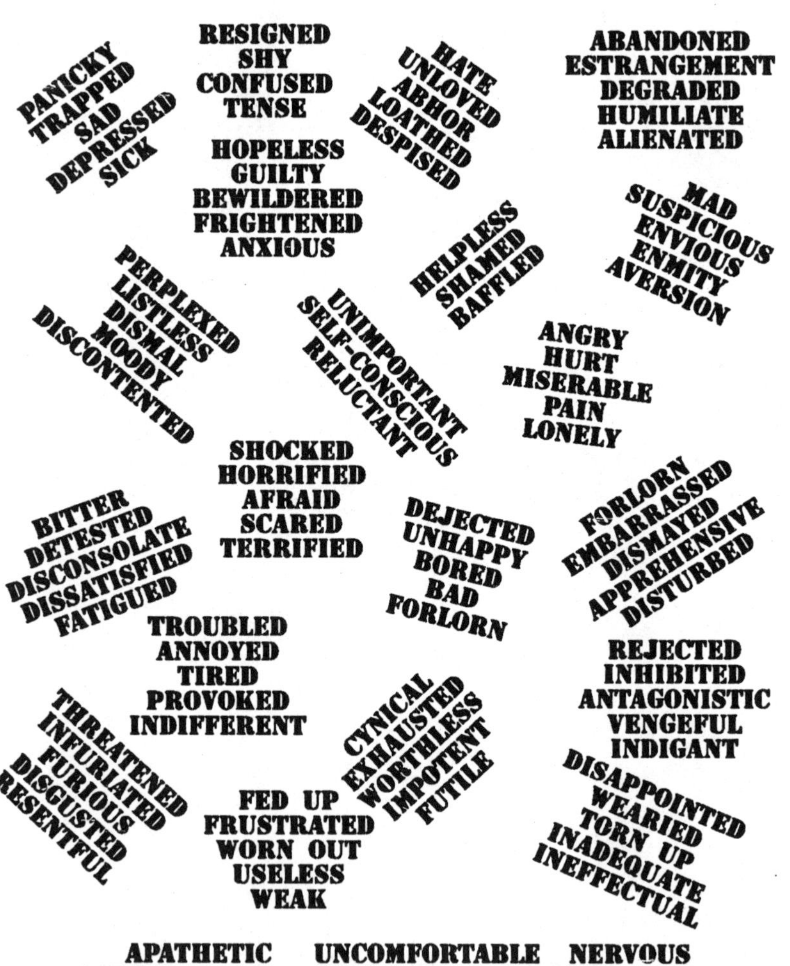

APATHETIC UNCOMFORTABLE NERVOUS
WORRIED CONTEMPTUOUS UNSURE ALARMED

used to help gain insight into the levels of intimacy that groups achieve, and processes that both facilitate and inhibit intimate verbal interaction. Specifically, the instrument can be used as:

1. A *guide* for group leaders to use in facilitating a group. A group leader who knows the LOVIT method will be able to talk in ways that produce levels of intimacy which are helpful to the group.

2. A *tool* for assessing group problems. A leader or the members of groups can examine the group's own conversation and identify particular patterns of development that seem to produce problems.

3. A *method for focusing interaction* in groups that have intimacy as a goal (such as marriage or friendship). Many kinds of groups are concerned with intimacy. Perhaps the group that talks most about intimacy is the marriage counseling group. In this group the members are usually trying to reach a level of intimacy that is satisfying to both partners. The LOVIT can be used to discover the levels that each partner uses, thus focusing on differences that exist between partners. It can help both partners determine methods for developing mutually satisfying levels of intimacy.

4. A *goal-setting device* for use in groups. If a group (a couple, training group, support group, etc.) identifies improvement of communication as a goal, members can use LOVIT to select specific intimacy patterns they wish to practice and achieve.

The LOVIT functions as a model for monitoring verbal behavior. Groups **and individuals** can monitor their own interaction and ask themselves whether they are operating at the levels they want. If not, why not? Only a group or person can really answer these questions, as well as use LOVIT as a tool which can make the questions more answerable.

One example of a specific exercise for using the intimacy categories follows. First, read the directions. After you have completed the rankings, discuss your responses with your partner.

Exercise: The Intimacy Style Analysis

The LOVIT includes descriptions that can be used to characterize statements made in a conversation. There are three columns for your responses. In column A, rank the items according to *your own use* of the behavior described in the item. Second, record your perception of your partner's behavior by ranking the items in column B. Use column C to record your ideas about what you would prefer in your relationship. All three rankings are done in the same way. If an item is most characteristic of you (column A), it would be ranked 1. If it's least characteristic, it would be ranked 10.

The third column is ranked according to the way you would like your relationship to be characterized. So you should place 1 before the item (behavior) you want most in your relationship, and a 10 for the item that you want least. Try to rank as many of the ten items as possible. Be sure to rank the categories/levels that are *most* and *least* important rather than being concerned with those behaviors in the "middle" which you do not see as crucial.

After you have ranked the categories for all three columns, share your rankings with your partner. The most important guide for this process is to *listen to the other person's rankings* and try to be sure you understand her/his perceptions accurately.

LEVELS OF VERBAL INTIMACY TECHNIQUE

A B C

❑ ❑ ❑ 1.No conversation

Time together without conversation. Silence, thinking, watching TV and reading. In a group, multiple conversation.

❑ ❑ ❑ 2.Small Talk

Talk about things that do not touch experience of those talking. Things that happen around us that we seem to have no control over. The weather, news and our interests. "How are you feeling? It is nice weather lately—I hope it lasts."

❑ ❑ ❑ 3. People in General

Includes characteristics, feelings, attitudes, principles and generalizations we make about individuals, groups, organizations and life. "People are afraid of violence—but in some way drawn to it."

❑ ❑ ❑ 4. Individual experience outside the relationship.
Experience in the life of one person that the other has not shared. "I met someone today who was so interesting—she and my sister talked for hours."

❑ ❑ ❑ 5. Conversation about others not present
Discussion refers to others close to those present but who are not present. May also be about some of those in the present group but not all. "I wish John were here."

❑ ❑ ❑ 6.Shared experience past or future
Talking about our past experience or our future experience or life. Includes ideas about the group or relationship in general. "We talked about that before."

❑ ❑ ❑ 7. Individual Experience, Feeling/Reaction
Feelings expressed by one person about his/her outside experience. "I feel bad about the way people acted in the meeting before I met you."

❑ ❑ ❑ 8. Indirect Expression of Feeling
Feeling expressed to the partner indirectly; through judgment, evaluation, tone of voice. "You really have a very unusual way of showing your superiority."

❑ ❑ ❑ 9.Description of Shared Experience

Talking about the relationship *without* the use of feelings, judgments or evaluations. "I noticed you haven't talked yet or looked at me."

❑ ❑ ❑ 10. Direct expression of Feeling

Feeling expressed to the partner so that it clearly identifies the speaker as having the feeling and does not judge or evaluate the partner. "I feel good and very happy about what you did."

Looking at Verbal Control

As we have said before, words are among the most useful tools we have. People in all situations talk to one another constantly. At times, messages are misunderstood. Misunderstanding leads to problems in the relationship as well as difficulty in achieving the goal of communication. Misunderstanding can produce conflict, and in the most extreme cases alienation, separation, isolation, and violence.

We communicate with each other primarily with the language that we use. The message that scientists have always had for us "...if we study it, we can improve it." Let us keep that message in mind as we explore the dimension of verbal control.

The Levels of Verbal Control Technique includes ten categories of behavior, largely verbal, which can be used to analyze the messages people send and the patterns of message exchange that develop when people are talking.

These categories of verbal behavior come from a number of different ideas related to the amount of authority or direction that is used in the message sent to another. How much direction, correction, focus, and criticism is included in the message? This is the focus for the categories. These ideas have been the concern of social scientists for many years. In applied fields of psychology, counseling and education, there has been particular interest in behavior teachers, group leaders, administrators and counselors of various kinds.

This discussion will not be an extensive review of different schemes for looking at leadership, power and authority. Rather, we simply acknowledge that our approach is not original but is modification of ideas, methods and procedures developed and refined by Flanders and his colleagues.(1)

The categories used here are designed specifically for the analysis of patterns of directiveness in verbal messages. The emphasis is on *understanding the pattern* that characterizes an exchange between people. The description of these patterns enables you to see consequences of particular direction and response patterns.

As you look at the categories, try to get an overall idea of the kinds of behavior and their order. Then memorize the categories in order, from Level 1 to Level 10. When they have been memorized, you can practice informally by just asking yourself as you listen to people talking, "What category of behavior is that?" After you have done this for a few times you will begin to see that patterns of control appear as people exchange verbal messages. With practice, you will become skilled at using this technique.

1 The work done by Flanders and others explored the concepts of directness, directiveness and relationships between the directiveness of leaders and reactions of group members.. The categories described in this section are based on Flanders' categories and can be viewed as a revision of Flanders' Interaction Analysis System.
For a review of this work see Amidon, Flanders and Casper (1985).

In the previous section the concept of directiveness was introduced. The presentation of a scale of categories or levels of directiveness will help to make this idea more concrete.

LEVELS OF
VERBAL CONTROL TECHNIQUE:
The Categories

Level 1 - Silence

This level is a non-talking category. It describes an uncertain condition of directiveness. It occurs when no one is talking or when several people are talking at once.

It is important to notice how long silence lasts in conversation. When do people fall silent? Silence has many meanings in a conversation. What is your reaction to silence? Some silent periods are very uncomfortable. Usually if you think carefully and objectively about what was said just before a silence, or what unusual patterns of conversation occurred before the silence, the meaning of the silence can become clear or at least some clues to its meaning will be uncovered.

In these periods of silence, people are usually thinking. In some sense this category allows for further analysis of the exchange of messages. When people are together and not talking, they are often thinking about what to say or what has been said. At times people are waiting for someone else to talk, or something to happen.

This level of behavior is used to make the continuum complete. That is, it makes the scheme useable at any time and in any situation where people are together. Silence is not a totally ambiguous class of behavior in terms of interpretation. During periods of silence people think, communicate nonverbally and generally send out and receive messages that may be seen as a part of the total communication pattern. When you use a method for analysis of directiveness in control behavior, the silence category may help in understanding overall patterns of control, resistance, conflict and resolution. A more complete analysis of the meaning of silence in communication patterns is presented later in this section. Nonverbal behavior is treated extensively in a later chapter.

Level 2 - Negative Reaction

Statements in this category include negative evaluation, criticism, reprimand, negative feelings, defensive behavior, and self-justification.

Criticism, reprimand, negative evaluation and expression of negative feelings are all considered *directive expression of control*. In what sense are these statements directive? Why are critical, negative, evaluative and reprimand statements so significant in a concept of power, control and authority?

When we think of control or power, we think of directive-oriented organizations. Historically, military, religious, corporate and governmental organizations operate on the principle of direction from the top down. The words used are most extreme when the direction or directiveness must be focused on errors, mistakes, or corrections. Statements of negative reaction or evaluation send the message that "your behavior is wrong, mistaken, erroneous or just unacceptable, and don't do it any more."

In a sense, negative evaluation or reaction is focused and directive in that it communicates what one must *not* do, and that doing certain things is not correct or appropriate.

Criticism is directive in that it indicates that there are limits, and that one must change behavior to fit the standards.

The reaction to criticism is frequently negative. It is often said that it's all right to criticize, but few like to be the recipients of criticism.

Often negative evaluation is expressed in such a way that it elicits a defensive reaction. When criticized, a person often feels defensive and at the same time feels that he/she *should not* feel defensive because the evaluating person is really "trying to help."

We associate evaluation with authority. Leaders of all kinds have as part of their roles the evaluation of their subordinates. When the subordinates do not meet standards, make mistakes, or perform inappropriately the authority or person in control criticizes or reprimands. It is particularly easy to see, therefore, that parents, teachers, managers, administrators, and officers of various types are critical and often directive.

Negative evaluation is something that can include a large element of non-talking behavior as well. The *tone of voice* can be the primary carrier of the question: "What are you doing?" This statement appears to be a request for information, but if it is said with a particular tone of voice the message is really: "What you are doing is wrong."

The eyes and the voice are both carriers of messages. Many people use the "stare" to communicate disapproval. The face is a powerful communicator of the message. A smile or lack of it can greatly change the meaning of the message, particularly if the words are strongly negative. Consider this example:

"You are making a big mistake. I think that you are wrong, and totally inappropriate. It's going to get you into a whole lot of trouble."

This message is sent with a smile. What does the receiver think and feel when the message is sent with a smile? First of all, the message is extremely direct. The person receiving can have little doubt about the desires of the person doing the reprimanding. There seems to be clarity about what the speaker *does not want* the receiver to do. But what about the smile? Its inclusion opens the message to interpretation. Does the smile mean that the critical message is not so critical, or does it mean the sender wants to include a positive message with the negative? Perhaps the greatest problem in this type of message is the possibility that the smile will confuse the receiver. For example, "perhaps the smile means that he is enjoying criticizing me." Of course there can be an unlimited number of meanings associated with any message. The more discrepant the words and the physical behavior, the more likely people are to receive a wide range of messages. A more extensive discussion of this topic is included in the section on nonverbal behavior.

Some of the messages classified in Category 2 include:

- *Stop doing that right now!*
- *Don't ever let me hear that again.*
- *I don't agree with that. It's very naive.*
- *I don't like what you did. I think it's stupid.*
- *I'm really angry. What are you doing?*
- *You are wrong in what you are doing.*
- *You're causing me trouble with what you're doing.*
- *If you do that again, it's the end of us.*
- *I'm a nobody, but you're a big shot.*
- *That's poor work.*
- *What in heaven's name is going on here?*
- *I'm so discouraged.*
- *I quit.*
- *It's no use, I can't do it.*
- *We failed.*
- *I'll never ask you to do something for me again.*

Level 3 - Corrective Feedback

Statements in this category give information. They tell you what you are doing that's wrong, why it's in error, and how to do it right or correct it. Level 3 is considered to be the next most directive category. It includes statements that send the following message(s):

a) Something is missing and/or some error has been made.

b) You need certain information to change or do it better.

c) This is the information you need.

d) This is why you need the information.

The statement does provide corrective information for the receiver in the sense that emphasis is placed on information rather than the error. The feedback given in correction allows the receiver to operate without greater or increased direction or criticism. Corrective feedback differs from the negative reaction in that the feedback is specific and focused on the reason for the correction. These statements may also differ from negative evaluation because of the lack of disapproval in the statement. This does not mean that corrective feedback is not often perceived as negative, rather that the emphasis in this category is on information: What is the error, and why it needs to be corrected. Some examples would be:

- *Wait, wait, put your hands down.*
- *Now again, louder. People in the back need to hear you.*
- *It's all OK except the last line.*
- *These eggs need more cooking.*
- *Please use less perfume next time.*
- *Your collar is up in back.*
- *I'd appreciate it if you would stop calling me Millie.*

- *Other members of the group have trouble getting a word in when you talk. Watch their faces.*
- *No, not there, up higher.*
- *You're all too anxious. Relax.*
- *Take it easy on that punch. It has to be enough for everyone.*

Level 4 - Direction, Instruction, Command

A direction is of course directive but does not in and of itself mean or communicate anything about something wrong, an error, or a mistake.

The direction leaves no doubt about what the speaker wants. The message of the direction is specific. Sometimes the direction includes specific details (when, where and how). Directions are often short and to the point:

- *Just wail till I'm done with this sentence and then I'll listen to you.*
- *Stop the car here and let me out.*
- *Go over to the table and get me that paper.*

These are specific statements that don't leave much room for confusion about what the speaker wants.

Sometimes the direction is specific about what action the speaker wants but is stated as a request rather than a command. For example:

- *Would you mind repeating that?*
- *Will you hand me the paper?*

The form is different but the focus of the direction is clear. Generally, a direction contains an action verb and includes the idea that if the person carries out the instruction, then one can see or hear the person following the direction.

Directions don't in and of themselves mean trouble for the sender or the receiver. They are not negative in and of themselves. But they may become negative if they are frequently used by one person in a relationship and not used, or infrequently used, by the other person(s). In an equal relationship, the unequal use of directions by one person in the relationship may produce resistance in the other. The real issues are when, how, where, how often, and to whom do you give directions? All of these should be considered in any analysis of directions.

Level 5 - Suggestion, Advice, or Wishes

Statements in this category often use words like you *could*, *should* or *ought to* do this or that. These statements are similar to directions but differ in that they are less specific. Often advice is given as a "wish" after something has happened:

- *I wish you had told me about that.*

The message that an advice or suggestion statement usually carries is you should try to do it another way. The *ought* or *should* is usually included in the statement or it is understood:

- *Buy from the supermarket. Don't go to the gourmet shop any more, it's too expensive.*

The "you should" is clearly a part of the message. Some people have suggested that advice and suggestions are really just indirect criticisms or directions:

- *Why don't you try taking the bus?*
- *You know I think you should have told him that.*
- *It ought to be easy for you to go back and ask for your money back.*
- *I think you could get a lot out of a course on 'how to get along with people'.*

Level 6 - Information, facts, opinions, ideas and thoughts about many things

This is a broad category, and includes much of what we talk about. It includes facts, ideas and opinions about almost everything. The general category that we call *knowledge* or *facts* is included here.

Another type of talk in this category is about life experiences or facts about one's life. Descriptions of how the person views things, or feels, is also included here.

Essentially, Level 6 emphasizes providing information. The information may either be about the speaker or it may be about some topic that is beyond the scope of the relationship or the situation. One question to use as a guide while using this category is:

Is the person just providing information to the other(s) present, or is the information embedded in a suggestion, evaluation, direction, correction or question?

If the statement gives information and not a suggestion, then it is information and only information. When information is embedded in a suggestion, question, evaluation, direction, or correction, it is probably functioning as another category. Examples of Level 6 statements include:

- *There are many things I'm interested in these days, mostly the world, people and my family. (Information about the speaker's life)*
- *I think that some sports or physical movement activity is useful for everyone. (The speaker's opinion)*
- *I just saw that the World Series game was rained out. (This is a fact about the outside world)*
- *I have one idea about why people are so reluctant to take part in political elections. (Some personal theory or hypothesis)*

Level 7 - Question for Information

The question is nearly as common as statements which give information. In some sense they go together.

- *Do you know anything about the new computers?*
- *What did you do after I left?*
- *What about the various energy sources? What sources are available?*

We know that a question is a question unless it fits one of the other categories as well. The question form may actually be used in any of the other categories, so that any question is not necessarily a Level 7 question.

In order for the statement to be considered a *real* question its message should be "I want to get some information about ____."

The real question clearly communicates that the speaker wants some facts, information or ideas:

- *What happened that seemed to produce the situation you described?*
- *What has been happening lately in your life?*
- *What can you tell me about the latest things that have been going on in your relationship?*
- *How do you react to situations that seem to drag on and on?*

Level 8 - Clarifying Question

A clarifying question is a specific type of question. It follows another person's statement. This is the kind of question that may follow a complicated point that someone has made. It is always made in response to a specific message that has been sent. The clarifying question is also fairly brief. The central message of this type of question is, "Can you clarify what you said?"

- *Were you saying you disagree or agree with me?*
- *Did you say to turn left or right?*
- *Are you saying you don't want to go?*

- *Did I hear you tell him you were angry or sad?*
- *Is that what you are saying?*
- *Could you explain that some more?*

Level 9 - Acknowledging the Contributions of Others

This category includes statements that summarize, restate, or simply refer to the contribution.

The central message in this kind of accepting or acknowledging statement is, "I am *listening*, understanding, and accepting your message. I am not evaluating it. It's OK with me the way it is."

Category 9 statements focus on and are responsive to the contribution. There are many sorts of statements that fall in this category. Generally they are short, not emotionally loaded, and introduce no new content to what the speaker has said:

- *I hear you.*
- *You seem to be upset.*
- *That sounds like you're really happy.*
- *I understand your point.*
- *OK.*
- *I'll think about your idea.*

Level 10 - Positive Reaction

The statements in this category are not directive to the speaker, but rather are responsive to him/her. The message is, "I like what you are saying. I like you, and your ideas are good."

In some sense Level 10 statements are the opposite of those in Level 2. Included are positive evaluation, praise, support and positive feeling.

The statements are not directive because they are focused on what the speaker is saying, and in fact *encourage the speaker to direct her/himself.*

This type of statement may be heard as "I am supporting you to go on and develop your ideas the way you are doing."

- *I really like what you did.*
- *I'm very attracted to you.*
- *What you are doing is important.*
- *Thanks a lot. I don't know how I could have done it without you.*

The ten levels of directiveness are all used by everyone to send messages of power and control at one time or another. We can ask ourselves as we talk:

1. How much negative reaction do I express in my relationships? What is the amount I want to send out? Do I express as much as I want to express?

2. In what situations do I give corrective feedback to others? How do I feel about the person I'm correcting? How do I feel about the person who is correcting me?

3. How personal are my "positive reactions?" Who do I react to positively? How often?

4. How much time do I spend listening? More than I spend talking?

The first three questions can be used with all categories. Question four concerns listening. Listening is important in a balanced relationship. Any analysis of the patterns of your or other's control will consider questions like these.

There are many different ways to use the categories in one's own life, in both work and social situations. Sometimes it's revealing to listen carefully to a conversation you are involved in and just informally keep track of which patterns of control are occurring.

Exercise: The Control Style Analysis

You may also use the categories to systematically diagnose your own and your partner's interaction patterns. Try the following procedure with a friend or companion with whom you have a close relationship.

The LOVCT contains ten descriptions that can be used to characterize statements made in a conversation. There are three columns for your response. In column A, rank the items according to *your own use* of the behavior that is presented and described in the item. Next, record your perception of your partner's behavior by ranking the items in column B. Use column C to record your ideas about what you would like to see happen in your relationship. All three rankings are done in the same way. If an item is most characteristic of you (column A) it would be ranked 1. If it's least characteristic it would be ranked 10.

The third column is ranked according to the way you would like your relationship to be characterized. So you should place 1 before the item (behavior) you want most in your relationship, and a 10 for the item that you want least. If possible, try to ranl all 10 behaviors indicated by the LOVCT levels. It is important to include those behaviors that you want *most* and *least,* so be sure that you rank at least a few at each end of the scale. *This is more important than including every single item in the 10 levels.*

LEVELS OF VERBAL CONTROL TECHNIQUE

A B C

❑ ❑ ❑ 1. No conversation
Time together without conversation. Silence, thinking, watching TV and reading. In a group, multiple conversation.

❑ ❑ ❑ 2. Negative Reaction
Judgments, evaluation, defense, criticism, feelings directed to the partner. "I don't like that sort of thing. It just causes problems and it's not wise."

❑ ❑ ❑ 3. Corrective Feedback
Information, facts that show how or where a person was in error or made a mistake. "If you had shown me the information I would have agreed with you."

❑ ❑ ❑ 4. Direction
Command, direction and instruction telling the other person to do something. "Now I want you to listen to me very carefully—let me finish before you respond."

- ❑ ❑ ❑ 5. Suggestion or Advice
  Suggestions offering the opinion that the other person should do something. "I think you should tell him how you feel. He needs to know."

- ❑ ❑ ❑ 6. Information, facts, opinions
  Information about anything that is just information without feeling. Talk in this category includes things outside our opinions and the facts about ourselves. All information that *does not* function as reaction feedback, direction, suggestion, question or acceptance is in this category.

- ❑ ❑ ❑ 7. Questions for Information
  Questions that ask the other person for information about anything. "What do you think about that? What are your ideas? What can you tell me about that?"

- ❑ ❑ ❑ 8. Questions for Clarification
  The question is focused on something the person just said. It is designed to check out or clarify what the other person said. "Are you saying that you agree with it but have some new ideas?"

- ❑ ❑ ❑ 9. Acknowledging, Attending, Accepting
  Statement that shows that the person is listening or attending to what the other person is saying.

❑ ❑ ❑ 10. Positive Reaction
Judgments, praise, support, feelings expressed to the partner. "I like that type of thing. It just helps the situation and it's very smart."

After you and your partner have ranked the three columns it is useful to be able to talk with your partner. This can be done in a variety of ways, but it is most important to *listen* to feedback and avoid argument. Discuss perceptions that you both have of your behavior, and any discrepancies in perception that are revealed by the exercise. Remember, your goal is to gain information about the way you talk to people in close relationships.

How Intimacy and Control Occur in Your Talking

No matter how we talk to others we affect them, and power and intimacy "messages" are communicated.

The LOVIT and LOVCT can help us monitor our own conversation as well as our own thoughts. Here we have only focused on our *talking* but later we will focus on our thinking as well.

In this section we will look at how our messages of power and intimacy are related to one another.

Each scale provides a way for classifying verbal statements. The intimacy level for a group of two or more persons is determined by looking at the LOVIT levels of statements made by everyone in the group. In a couple, for example, if one person makes Level 10 statements and the other responds with Level 3 statements, the conversation is not very intimate. If both people were talking at Levels 9 and 10 the conversation would be really intimate. The highest intimacy levels occur when the conversation from *all participants* is taking place in the higher intimacy categories (6, 7, 8, 9, 10).

The control system is similar. If control is exercised by one person using the directive categories, (2-5) and the other person is using the responsive categories (6-10), there is not much reciprocity in the control process. Similarly, if both persons tried to control the other with talk, this indicates high levels of directive control and is predictive of conflict. However, if both tend to use responsive control statements (6-10), the conversation indicates egalitarian or shared control processes in their interactions.

Conversation is described as being at a *particular level* of intimacy when both members of a couple are saying things that fall in the same category (or categories).

A conversation is described as a *particular level* of control in a similar way, with speakers tending to share the same category or categories.

Looking at the average level of participant's statements is meaningless. Rather consider the pattern of levels of control or intimacy.

Most often, talk in couples and groups is not at a particular level. It has to be described by the patterns and sequences of talk. These are often revealing and become easy to identify with practice.

A Look Upward

Much of self-to-self interaction is hidden from the outside world. We are aware of others' self-talk only when it is verbalized:

- *I'm really upset with myself.*
- *I can't seem to get going.*

These two examples are relatively direct. Often, even what friends say about their own thoughts is expressed to us indirectly. We have an especially good opportunity to look at the ways others interact with us using the control-intimacy concepts. Generally there is a predictable relationship between intimacy and control. That is, when a person's control style is directive with another person, then his/her intimacy style is a fairly distant one.

Perhaps the generalization about intimacy and control with others that covers almost all situations is that directiveness and closeness exist together when members of a group accept a model of control in which a designated person or persons exert(s) directive control. That is, a situation of shared or agreed upon use of power exists which permits intimacy to flourish. The reason that many of our social experiences are lacking in intimacy is that the issues of power and control are still being worked on.

How do we exercise control in our relationships through talking? Think about the following examples and the control message you get from each statement:

- *Come over and see me and we will talk.*
- *I have some good ideas for you.*
- *No, don't do that, I don't want that type of thing.*
- *I can help you with that problem.*
- *I like to work with you. I don't mind explaining it to you.*

In the case of these examples the intimacy message seems submerged or at least delayed. That is, it "hasn't been sent yet."

All of these statements may include an important message about control and power. What is it, and what does it have to do with intimacy?

Maybe the speaker is "above" (symbolic of directive control) you. So what does the control message do for the intimacy message that is also there?

- *I'd like to talk some more with you.*
- *I'd like to get to know you better.*
- *What you say sounds interesting.*

The control message we can send which does not interfere with intimacy messages is the message of equality. This is a message that says "I will try to stay *with* you, not over you." Messages about control over another person can produce a resistance to intimacy.

Thinking Exercise

This exercise may be valuable for times when a partner is not available, or when you choose to look at a relationship to clarify your own thinking about it:

1. Write down your thoughts about the conversation that occurs in a relationship you consider close.

2. Notice which levels of LOVIT and LOVCT scales describe the conversation.

3. Imagine a pattern of interaction or conversation which would produce a more satisfying control and/or intimacy pattern.

4. Try to develop a strategy for talking with your partner in the relationship about the issues that come up for you in this exercise.

Can the LOVIT and LOVCT be applied to you and me? Another way of asking this question is, do we want to focus on the way we talk using the framework of closeness and/or control? We can increase this awareness in ourselves, and some of the discomfort we feel can be replaced by insight. The goal of this chapter is to help a person understand his/her role in the communication that characterizes an important relationship. The tools presented can be used to help each individual understand what is needed to make the interactions more satisfying for the people involved in the talk and the relationship.

CHAPTER 4

How the Conversation Categories May Be Used

There are at least four main ways that the categories of intimacy and control may be used:

1. To become more personally aware of what we say and think, and how this may affect others.

2. To understand more clearly what is happening in a group we are leading, teaching, training or facilitating.

3. To train individuals or groups in verbal skills.

4. To carry out data collection for research on couples or groups.

"You don't know what you're saying!" is not just a line from old plays and movies. It's an expression that describes most people. We are simply not very aware of the probable effects on others of what we say. An extreme example is a parent who may give "double-bind" messages (do this/don't do this) to a child, which produces confusion and possibly emotional disorder. A more common occurrence is seen in marriages where mates are not very aware of how much criticism they communicate to one another, so the relationship becomes distant and unhappy. As a matter of fact, most people would be surprised (and maybe embarrassed) to see what their patterns of verbal intimacy and control are when they talk informally with others.

If you are aware of the categories, and are thus more aware of your patterns of intimacy and control as you speak to other people, you will have greater freedom and flexibility in deciding to change your behavior. You can have different kinds of relationships with others. You also may use the categories to *monitor* and better understand your own thoughts: "What messages am I sending myself today?"

The categories for both the Intimacy Technique and Control Technique are presented here and are referred to throughout this chapter.

Thoughts May be Categorized as Well as Conversation

These two observation techniques were developed for primarily for use with conversation. This remains their primary application. They may be used as well with thoughts, which may be considered "internal conversations" or self-talk.

Becoming more aware of one's own thought and speaking patterns by using the LOVIT and LOVCT can be accomplished independently, without the aid of another person. It is possible to analyze one's own conversation while it is taking place. The difficulty with this method is that it means attending to two things at the same time. This seems all right for short periods, but it would probably be difficult to do at all times. One way to use the categories while interacting is simply to ask the question, "Am I doing what I want?" Ask this as soon after a conversation as possible, use the categories on your own thoughts. Thoughts - internal conversation - can be classified using the LOVIT and LOVCT.

We seldom "take our thoughts out of our head." We hardly ever look at them with the same objectivity and with the same perspective we would if they were some one else's, analyzing them, and seeing what we can do about them.

Thoughts are creative. That is, every thought we have produces an effect in *us*, on our *actions*, or on our immediate *environment*. We don't need to take an extreme position to illustrate the point that hearing and understanding our own thoughts clearly is an important approach or first step to gaining perspective on our own behavior. Most people have had some experiences with the creative effects of thoughts.

If you make an error that costs you something, you probably get angry with yourself. The thought may seem harmless, as in "my carelessness made me lose ten dollars." But the thought really said to you that your carelessness hurt you. And your next thought may be, "I don't take good care of things important to me." And your next thought may be, "Everything goes wrong, so why bother?" There is even a negative "law of life" which states that "If anything can go wrong it will." These thoughts or internal messages may then actually increase the carelessness that upsets you and produce another accident. When you believe that you can't do anything right, your thoughts may be directing your actions toward that reality.

LEVELS OF VERBAL INTIMACY TECHNIQUE (LOVIT)

❑ ❑ ❑ 1.No conversation

Time together without conversation. Silence, thinking, watching TV and reading. In a group, multiple conversation.

❑ ❑ ❑ 2.Small Talk.

Talk about things that do not touch experience of those talking. Things that happen around us that we seem to have no control over. The weather, news and our interests. "How are you feeling? It is nice weather lately — I hope it lasts."

❑ ❑ ❑ 3.People in General.

Includes characteristics, feelings, attitudes, principles and generalizations we make about individuals, groups, organizations and life. "People are afraid of violence — but in some way drawn to it."

❑ ❑ ❑ 4. Individual experience outside the relationship.

Experience in the life of one person that the other has not shared. "I had met someone today that was so interesting — she and my sister talked for hours."

❑ ❑ ❑ 5. Member shared experience outside group.
Discussion refers to others close to those present but not present. May also be about experience shared outside the group by some of those in the present group but not all. "I wish John were here."

❑ ❑ ❑ 6. Shared experience past or future.
Talking about our past experience or our future experience or life. Includes ideas about the group or relationship in general. "We talked about that before."

❑ ❑ ❑ 7. Individual Experience, Feeling Reaction.
Feelings expressed by one person about his/her outside experience. "I feel bad about the way people acted in the meeting before I met you."

❑ ❑ ❑ 8. Indirect Expression of Feeling.
Feeling expressed to the partner indirectly; through judgment, evaluation, tone of voice. "You really have a very unusual way of showing your superiority."

❑ ❑ ❑ 9. Description of Shared Experience.
Talking about the relationship *without* the use of feelings, judgments or evaluations. "I noticed you haven't talked yet or looked at me."

❑ ❑ ❑10. Direct Expression of Feeling.

Feeling expressed to the partner, so that it clearly identifies the speaker as having the feeling and does not judge or evaluate the partner. "I feel good and very happy about what you did."

LEVELS OF VERBAL CONTROL TECHNIQUE (LOVCT)

❑ ❑ ❑ 1. No Conversation.
Time together without conversation. Silence, thinking, watching TV and reading. In a group, multiple conversation.

❑ ❑ ❑ 2. Negative Reaction.
Judgments, evaluation, defense, criticism, feelings directed to the partner. "I don't like that sort of thing. It just causes problems and it's not wise."

❑ ❑ ❑ 3. Corrective Feedback.
Information, facts that show how or where person was in error or made a mistake. "If you had shown me the information I would have agreed with you."

❑ ❑ ❑ 4. Direction.
Command, direction and instruction telling the other person to do something. "Now I want you to listen to me very carefully — let me finish before you respond."

❑ ❑ ❑ 5. Suggestion or Advice.
Suggestions offering the opinion that the other person should do something. "I think you should tell him how you feel. He needs to know."

❑ ❑ ❑ 6. Information, facts, opinion.
Information about anything that is just information without feeling. Talk in this category includes things outside our opinions and the facts about ourselves. All information that *does not* function as reaction, feedback, direction, suggestion, question or acceptance is in this category.

❑ ❑ ❑ 7. Questions for Information.
Questions that ask the other person for information about anything. "What do you think about that? What are your ideas? What can you tell me about that?"

❑ ❑ ❑ 8. Questions for Clarification.
The question is focused on something the person just said. It is designed to check out, or clarify what the other person said. "Are you saying that you agree with it but have some new ideas?"

❑ ❑ ❑ 9. Acknowledging, Attending, Accepting.
Statement that shows that the person is listening or attending to what the other person is saying.

❑ ❑ ❑ 10. Positive Reaction.
Judgments, praise, support, feelings expressed to the partner. "I like that type of thing. It just helps the situation and it's very smart.

Exercise: What Are My Thoughts Doing To Me?

Some of us have difficulty understanding the messages our thoughts are sending to us. Becoming aware takes practice, and one of the best ways to start is to learn to talk to yourself. This exercise can increase the awareness of your thoughts.

1. Either write down your thoughts or say them into a tape recorder. Continue doing this for 5 minutes. Continue writing or saying them even if you cannot make sense out of them.

2. Space your thoughts out. That is, leave space between separate thoughts. If you are taping your thoughts, pause between them. If writing, leave space on the paper between thoughts.

3. After you have recorded your thoughts for five minutes, go back over them and try to classify them using the LOVIT and LOVCT.

4. If possible, meet with a partner and compare your thoughts with the other person's thoughts. You may skip this step if you are doing the exercise by yourself.

5. Notice the patterns of intimacy and control that are contained in your thoughts.

Consider the following example:

LOVIT Category		LOVCT Category
8	I wish Paul wouldn't get so excited.	2
8	If he could just be quieter, other kids would like him better.	3
8	I don't spend enough time with him. He's only nine.	2
8	I wish he wouldn't talk now.—Shut up!	2
10	I guess I can understand him wanting attention and feeling excited about the world series. I really feel better about it if I think about it as a "once in a lifetime" thing.	9

In this example, worry, guilt, and judgment are expressed in terms of the control techniques of criticism, correction, and judgment expressed both toward the thinker himself and the person being thought about.

The internal messages here are focused on control of the other person and the self. The thinker is thinking, "I want to change the other (Paul), and if I am different it may affect him." The message underlying this may be, "I am not OK. Paul and I need to change."

The intimacy messages begin with the awareness of bad feelings. The final message seems to be, however, "Perhaps I can accept him (Paul's behavior) if I have more perspective and understanding." However, there is no clear self-accepting thought message here.

By going through the process of (1) identifying your thoughts, (2) analyzing them and (3) recognizing their effects, it is possible to get an idea of how your thoughts affect your perceptions, attitudes and behavior.

Going through this procedure does not necessarily mean that you are going to get everything you want from your thought processes. It is necessary to gradually increase the (self) control we have over our thoughts. The first step is developing *awareness.* The central question here seems to be, "How can we have the kinds of thoughts that bring about or create what we want?"

How to Record and Interpret Information

In the previous chapter a description and explanation of the procedure for using the categories of intimacy and control was presented. Although these categories have been used most often as a way of analyzing conversation between two or more people, the first example given in this chapter was an application of the categories to the analysis of one's own thoughts. This next example represents a much more typical use of the categories. The explanation which follows the example will show how discussion in a group can be systematically recorded (coded), and then how the information thus generated is summarized, organized and interpreted.

Figure 1 is a tally sheet used to record the categories of conversation when you are observing group interaction. The rows represent the 10 LOVIT categories, and the columns represent units of time. Each cell (square) represents 30 seconds' worth of tallies, so that two cells represent a minute's worth of interaction time. Each cell can contain up to three tally marks.

Each tally represents 10 seconds of observed interaction time. All tally entries are made sequentially, from left to right, so it is possible to trace the sequence of interaction as well. For example, it is possible to trace the conversation from category to category as it occurs over approximately a seven minute period.

Look at the illustration to see how one observer might code a seven minute conversation. The discussion starts out in category 5, goes to 4, and then back to 5 (in column 1) then to 6 (in column 2). The conversation ends in category 10 (column 14).

Figure 1
Seven Minutes of Interaction LOVIT Categories

LOVIT CATEGORIES	1	2	3	4	5	6	7	8	9	10	11	12	13	14	TOTAL
1. Silence															
2. Small Talk. Discussion unrelated to any group															
3. People in general. Discussion related to group phenomenon															
4. Individual Experience	|														
5. Part of Group	| |							|	|						
6. Shared experience - past & future		| | |						|	|						
7. Individual Experience Feelings			|					|	|						
8. Indirect expression of feelings			| |	| | |			| |			|					
9. Description of present					| |		|			|	|		|		
10. Direct expression of feelings					|	| | |				|	| |	| | |	| |	| | |	
	3	3	3	3	3	3	3	3	3	3	3	3	3	3	

Step By Step Instructions For Coding Conversation

1. Listen to the conversation until the context is clear and you have a good idea about what is going on (about 5 to 10 minutes).

Seven minutes ...

2. When you have achieved an understanding about what is going on, decide on a starting point. Listen to ten seconds of conversation after the starting point, and then classify this 10 seconds' worth of conversation into the appropriate category. This is done by locating the appropriate category row and inserting a tally mark in the *first third* of column one in the appropriate category row. The act of recording the tally in the appropriate row and column is allowed to take about ten seconds, so that at the end of the first ten seconds of coding time you will have made a decision, recorded one tally and are ready to listen to ten more seconds of conversation. Using this procedure, you listen for 10 seconds and enter a tally in the appropriate place. Each tally represents ten seconds of conversation. During the first ten seconds of a coding interval the observer listens, and in the second 10 seconds (s)he records a tally mark in the appropriate place.

3.The second tally mark is entered after listening to ten more seconds of talking. Again, the observer records the tally in the appropriate category row but this time places the tally in the *middle third* of column one.

4.The third entry is made in the same way, except that it will be placed in the appropriate category row in the *last one-third* of column one.

5.The fourth tally is recorded in the same way in the left hand one-third of column two. Continue to record tallies for each 10 seconds of conversation observed. Remember that each column contains three tallies and each tally represents ten seconds. Therefore each column represents thirty seconds' worth of tallies, and two columns together account for one minute's worth of time.

Mapping Sequences of Interaction

If we were to connect each tally on the sheet, we would actually produce a simple line graph that *defines the flow of conversation in terms of time and level of intimacy.* This is illustrated in Figure 2.

Another way to summarize information collected with the LOVIT or LOVCT is to total the tallies in each category for each of several meetings, and see if an overall trend develops from meeting to meeting.

Figure 2
Line Graph Connecting Each "Tally" for the Seven Minute Period

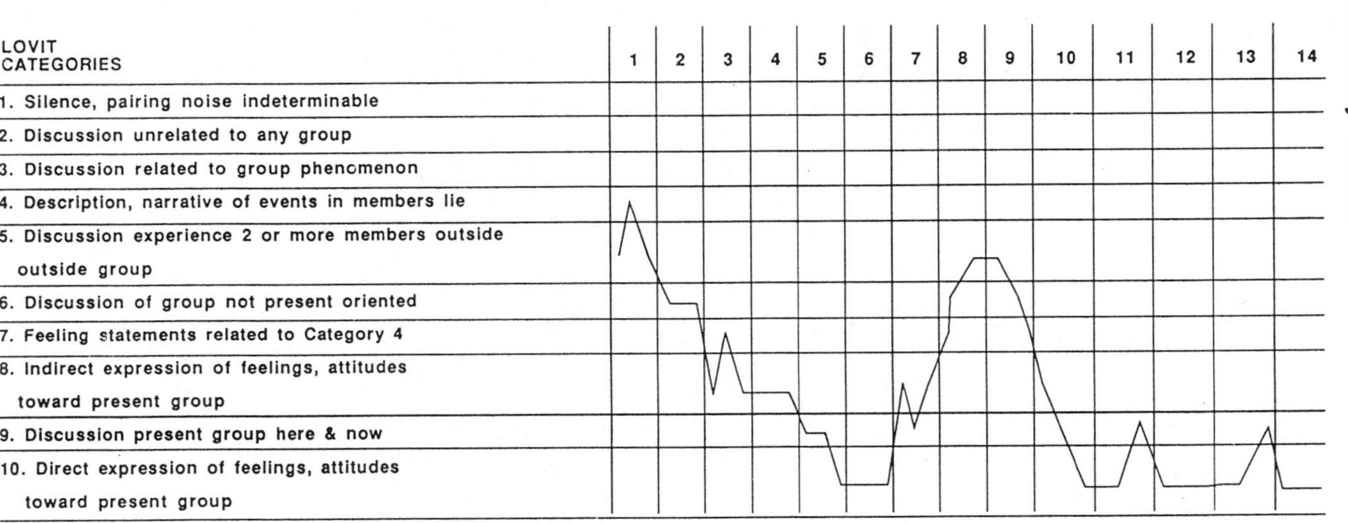

An example will show how this may be done. Let's say that you have seven minutes of interaction coded for the middle parts of seven different meetings. We know this is just a sample of the total interaction in an hour meeting, but perhaps even a few minutes will reveal trends in the patterns of intimacy or control.

In Figure 3 we see the actual number of entries in the LOVIT categories for seven different consecutive observations of a group. Since each session was observed for exactly seven minutes and six tallies are recorded in each minute, the total number of tallies in each session (column) will be 42. We can see the actual number of tallies and the midpoint (median) for each session presented in Figure 3. The median is a point which divides the information in half. If you look at the tallies in Figure 3, you will see that roughly half the tallies fall above the midpoint and the other half below the midpoint in each column.

In Figure 4 we see that a trend toward less intimacy developed in the first three meetings, and then a trend toward greater intimacy described in the last four meetings. Straight lines connecting the midpoints of the seven sessions illustrate these trends.

Figure 3
Sample of Seven Meetings

LOVIT CATEGORY	1		2		3		4		5		6		7	
	*	**	*	**	*	**	*	**	*	**	*	**	*	**
1. Silence														
2. Discussion unrelated to any group					4		4							
3. Discussion related to group phenomenon			3		15		4							
4. Description, narrative of events in members lie	4		4		10	X	2		4					
5. Discussion experience 2 or more members outside outside group	4		3		4		6		4		4		2	
6. Discussion of group not present oriented	5		6		10		10	X	10		10		10	
7. Feeling statements related to Category 4	3		9	X	2		5		4		2			
8. Indirect expression of feelings, attitudes toward present group	8	X	20				4		6	X	10	X	4	
9. Discussion present group here & now	6						4		8		15		10	X
10. Direct expression of feelings, attitudes toward present group	15						6		9		4		19	

*Total tally
** Midpoint (median tally)

Figure 4
Line Graph Connecting the Midpoints in Seven Meetings

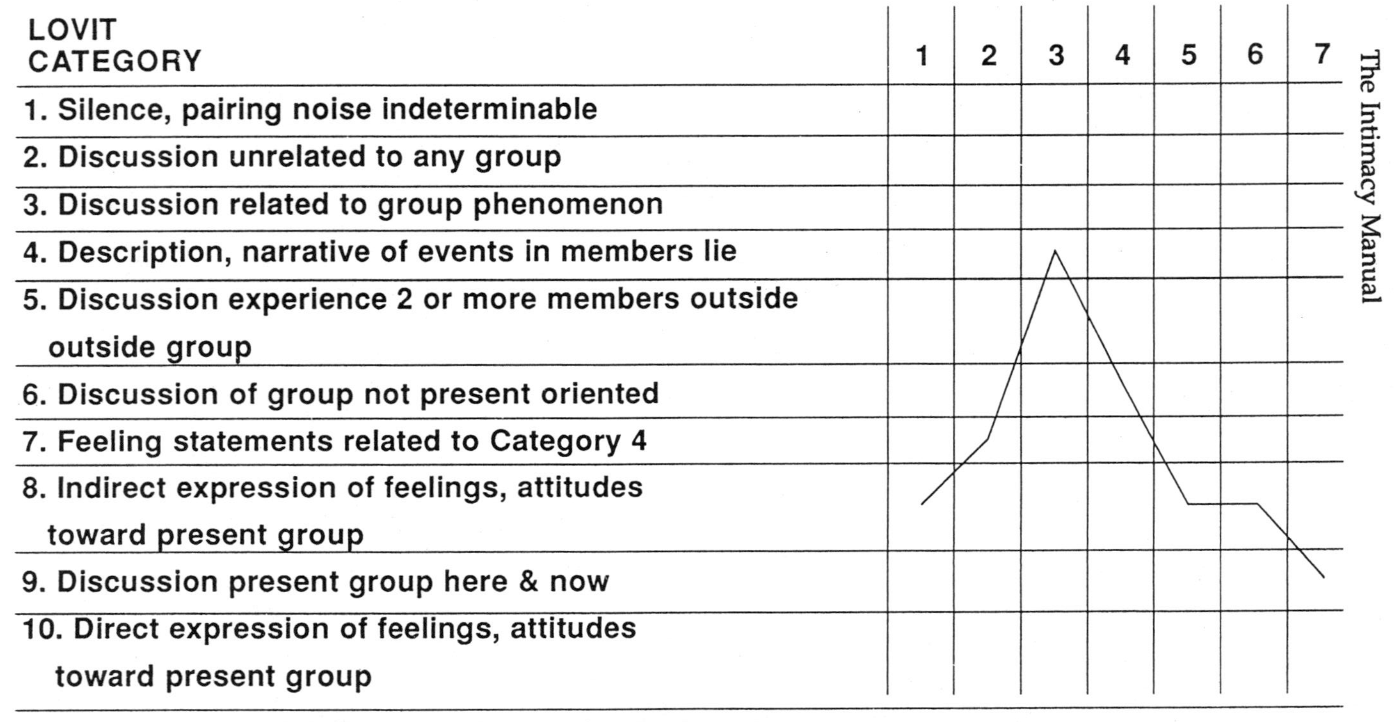

So far we have illustrated the tallying procedure for coding the LOVIT categories. The same procedure applies to the LOVCT. An example with the control technique may suggest ways that the *interpretation of information* gathered with the LOVCT is different from intimacy data gathered using the LOVIT.

In the example in Figure 5 we see that the conversation starts out in LOVCT category 6. It then moves up to five, four, three and eventually category two. It stays up in this area (categories two and three) for most of the next three minutes. Near the end of the seven minutes, the conversation included talk that was coded mostly in categories six and ten.

Figure 6 is similar to Figure 2 in that it illustrates how the pattern of control developed over seven minutes of observed interaction.

What can be done with these tallies? Well, several questions about the talk during those seven minutes may be answered. For example, which were the most frequently used control categories? What was the average or middle level of talk? What combinations in sequence were used more than once? These are some of the questions we could answer about any conversation. These questions may be answered by inspection (looking at the patterns) or by simple calculation of the midpoint.

Figure 5
Seven Minutes of Interaction
LOVCT Categories

LOVCT CATEGORIES	1	2	3	4	5	6	7	8	9	10	11	12	13	14
1. Silence														
2. Negative Reaction			I I	I I I	I	I	I I I							
3. Corrective Feedback			I		I			I I I						
4. Direction		I												
5. Suggestion		I I			I	I I								
6. Information	I I I									I I	I I I		I	
7. Question for Information									I I I					
8. Question Clarification										I				
9. Ackowledgement												I I		
10. Positive Reaction												I	I I	I I I
	3	3	3	3	3	3	3	3	3	3	3	3	3	

Figure 6
Line Graph Each Tally 7 Minute Period LOVCT Categories

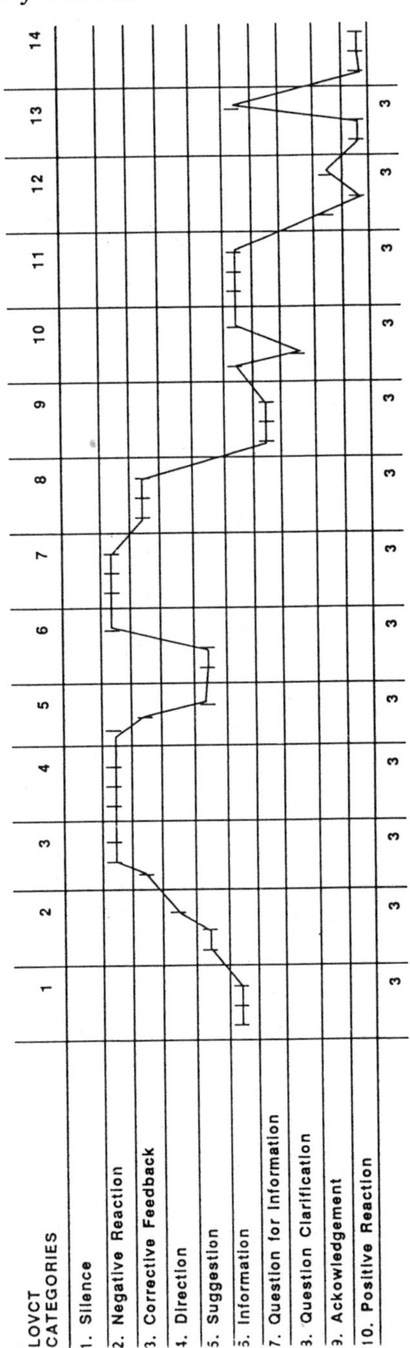

Six questions are basic to understanding both intimacy patterns and control patterns. When you look at the data you have collected, ask yourself:

1 How much conversation time is spent in each category?

2. What is the average level (mean or median) of the conversation on either the intimacy or control categories?

3. What are the combinations of categories used? Do they appear to indicate patterns of interaction?

4. Are there differences in intimacy and control patterns shown by the various participants in the conversation?

5. Is there a common conversation pattern that is similar to both (all) individual pattern(s)?

6. If individual patterns are different, how do they differ from one another?

If questions are raised about the verbal intimacy of the group in general, then other samples of talk are needed to form a basis for generalization. If we ask questions about some particular kind of group (e.g. people in group therapy), then samples of more than one such group would be needed as a beginning basis for that kind of conclusion. Similar work can be done with the LOVCT to look at control in couple or group talk.

Other Uses For The Category Systems

You may use LOVIT and LOVCT to look at yourself and decide if changes in your thinking and talking habits would benefit you:

1. Think of how you usually talk with friends in an informal setting. In which intimacy and control categories would you like to increase or decrease your talk?

2. Remember how your idle thoughts typically go when you are not occupied with something. What kind of control change would you like in your self talk? What kind of intimacy change would you like?

We have suggested that understanding what is going on along the two dimensions of intimacy and control allows us to understand a great deal of what is important in knowing the group. Knowing the two category systems allows the person in charge of a group's education, training or personal growth to be aware, with precision, of the level and movement of group talk. Interventions can then be made based on clear knowledge. Awareness of the category systems will also help the leader make such interventions as *modeling* a specific kind of verbal behavior and giving *feedback* to the group members about their own talk.

The way we grow up and are schooled, we usually get more experience and training in using categories 2-5 of the intimacy and control systems than we do for categories 6-10. So it is harder and does not seem as natural for us to express our feelings directly to another person ("I feel lonely tonight.") or to listen and accept what the other is saying ("I hear what you're saying"). It is easier to be indirect ("Look at all those lonely people!"). After a leader has discovered the levels of talk that seem to be lacking in a group's repertoire, exercises can be designed to focus on those levels, either one by one or in simple combinations. Consider this training exercise:

Three people get together (break down larger groups into subgroups of three) to talk two at a time, with the third person listening carefully. The task each time is for the two designated talkers to try to speak to each other in certain categories.

For example, if assigned control categories 6-8-9, the first speaker provides information (C6),the second speaker would ask a clarifying question (C8), and then the first speaker would respond with a statement of acknowledgement (C9). The pattern is then repeated with speakers switching roles. Some other patterns to practice would include Control 6-9, repeated, Intimacy 7-10 repeated; Intimacy 9-9-9-9, repeated. After each pattern has been completed, the listener can tell each participant whether or not (s)he accomplished the pattern. Roles can then be changed for two more rounds so that each person has the opportunity to speak and to listen.

A lot of the research on couples and groups has something to do with control (authority, influence, power) and intimacy (closeness, self-disclosure). The category systems offer a way of collecting data. For example, one study asks whether, men and women typically talk in different ways, in close relationship situations such as marriage counseling and (group dynamics) training groups. Some specific questions raised by this study include the following:

1. Do women talk *more* than men?

2. Are women more *self-disclosing* (verbally intimate) than men?

3. When men talk, do their remarks have more to do with directive control in relationships?

4. Do questions 1- 3 have different answers depending on the gender of the counselor or leader?

The talk in several groups and counseling sessions has been recorded and analyzed using the LOVIT and LOVCT.

To illustrate one way that this may be done for counseling sessions, the following short sample of conversation (not a part of the study) is offered:

Wife:

We are simply not getting along *at all* ...that's why we came. (Silence)

Counselor;
Do you agree with that?

Husband:

Well, I came because she kept insisting.

Wife:
It's not just me, we...(begins to cry a little)

Husband:
Alice, you know I can't stand it when you cry.

Counselor:
Perhaps if you would each tell me something about how you feel, that would be a good place to start.

If each remark is coded on the scales, the analysis looks like this:

	LOVIT Category	LOVCT Category
Wife	6	6
Counselor	6	7
Husband	6	6
Wife	8	6
Husband	8	2
Counselor	10	5

When the full analysis is made, tally-counts, averages or percentages can be computed to help answer questions about relative amounts of time spent in intimacy categories and power or control categories. A count of how many times (or minutes) the wife or husband talks provides information to answer the question of who talks more. Comparison of couples' conversations with male and female counselors begins to answer the question about the effect of counselor gender. To obtain reliable and generalizable answers to the questions we previously posed, you would need to study the conversations of a number of couples who had been selected for representativeness, and use more advanced statistical treatment of the results than has been suggested here. (If you want only the answers for a specific couple or a particular session the extra work isn't necessary, of course).

The systems are also meant to be used with couples and other groups of two(dyads). Two adjustments must be made in the Intimacy categories for use with dyads:

Level 4:
This talk has to do with the life experience of one person, not shared by the other.

Level 5:
This talk has to do with experiences one of the persons has had with another person who also has some relationship with the other person in the twosome.

The category systems may also be used in other ways. For example, a researcher or other person may directly observe a group in action and systematically collect data about the groups intimacy behavior. Using a coding sheet such as Figure 7 on the next page, the observer can follow the procedure outlined in the section of this chapter entitled *How to Record and Interpret Information.* Control behavior may be systematically studied in the same way.

Messages and Affirmations

We have explored some ideas for using the categories of intimacy and control that were presented in the previous chapter. LOVIT and LOVCT can be used best when the observer (data collector) is able to watch and listen to people as they interact. This can be done as a live observation or by using a high quality audio or video tape recording.

We have suggested some ways that these categories may be used to analyze one's own thoughts. In fact, this double use of the categories with thoughts (conversation with oneself) and with conversation with others is likely to produce the clearest understanding of our own messages about intimacy and control. This chapter contains a strong emphasis on analysis of thoughts and talking, but it has also included a discussion of "coding" verbal interaction and one of changing our thoughts so that they produce the desired results.

Figure 7
Coding Sheet
LOVIT Categories

	1	2	3	4	5	6	7	8	9	10	11	12	13	14
1. No conversation														
2. Small talk														
3. People in general														
4. Individual experience														
5. Conversation about those not present														
6. Shared experience Past or Future														
7. Individual experience Feeling reaction														
8. Indirect expression of feelings														
9. Description of Shared experience														
10. Direct expression of feeling														

We have raised issues about the nature of messages. Some ideas for thinking about the sources of messages have been presented. We are also considering the relationship of interaction (both interpersonal and intrapersonal) to the content of the message that is *received*.

The Nature of Messages

Approaches to the study of messages include consideration of their origin, meaning, and effect. Since all messages must be processed by the listener, self-messages may seem more important than messages sent to others.

We can think of messages as being in four areas, pictured as concentric circles.

The center circle represents the self, and includes messages from the self; the next level of relationship includes messages from one's primary relationship or important group, such as the family; next is the area of more casual contacts; and finally, the larger environment that is most vividly illustrated by the messages from the media, such as television.

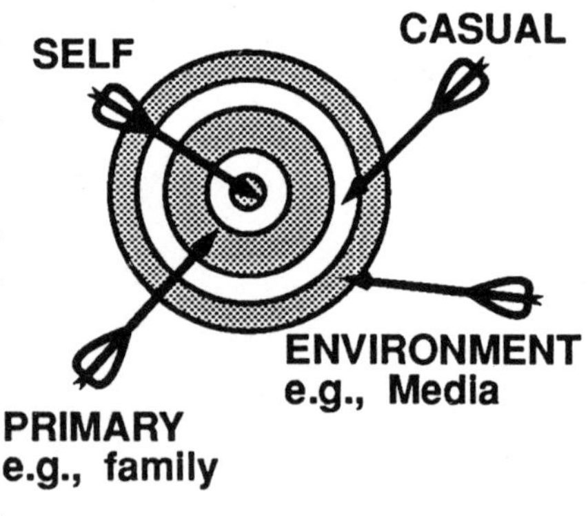

The *content* of messages can also be thought of as falling in one of the four concentric circles. Messages may be about (1) the self, (2) one's closest relationships, (3) friends and acquaintances or (4) the outside world.

Self-messages

The most important of all messages are those that have to do with us, and the most important *source* for each person is him/herself.

This diagram may illustrate the importance of messages in our lives. Think about the innermost circle. On a "good day," we might send ourselves the messages like, "I'm okay, things are going well, I can do the job, I'm going to get along just fine."

The significant people in our lives also send the messages that are positive, that support and reinforce our positive self-messages.

As we go through our day, people respond to us and generally will validate our good self feelings. Even when the news from the media is bad we are able to receive a positive message from and about ourselves, for example, "Some people are having a tough time but I have good control over my life."

One conclusion from this little exercise is that the *self* is a *source* of the message. It is clear that the four sources of messages are related to one another in that messages from all sources are processed by the self. In this sense, even though we cannot control the messages sent to us by the media, we process them and give them meaning for ourselves and our lives.

The job of the self, then, is message control. Messages need to be sent and received in such a way that they facilitate a person's most effective operation. The *affirmation* technique is a method that can be used to help control the effects of messages, and is especially useful in changing unwanted internal messages.

An affirmation is a positive statement about ourselves and our lives. It is a statement that sends a message from the self to the self. It may be stated in very specific, practical, operational language or it may use theoretical, general language. Most important, the message of the affirmation is from you to you so it needs to be stated in language you will use most effectively.

The general purpose of all affirmations is to provide an attitude that is conducive to accomplishment of goals. In order to do this it may be necessary to consider both specific and general affirmations. Some general affirmations that are applicable to most people include the message that, "I can do those things. I am able to make myself happy and successful." Key words in the affirmation process include: *I can, am able, now, do.*

There are other words equally as important which can guide you in developing an appropriate affirmation. These are negation words: *can't, don't, not, won't, and shouldn't.*

The negation words help define the nature of the problem that the self has.

The Use of the Negative

Not much has been written about the use of the negative and its effects on the self, but negation has a clear use in the affirmation process. Some would suggest, for example, that the way to develop affirmations is simply to identify one's negative messages and then reverse them so that they become positive messages to the self. Some simple examples come immediately to mind:

"I don't feel well ,and I don't know what's wrong. I can't do anything about it."

The reversal of this message could be:

"I don't feel as well as I'd like, but I know what's wrong. I can make myself feel better."

The primary use of the negative thought message is to identify the target area for an affirmation. What sort of affirmation do I need at this time? The negative can pinpoint the feelings toward which the affirmation needs to be directed.

Once the target area has been identified, the affirmation can be developed. It may be a simple reversal of the negative message. At times it is necessary to develop an affirmation that is seemingly unrelated to the negative message. Let's consider an example:

"I don't want to go to work, meet people or have any contact with the outside world."

The obvious reversal ("I want to go to work, meet people, and have contact with the outside world.") may be seen as a simple trick on the self that will not work. To bypass resistance, a more realistic affirmation can be formed:

"I know I feel bad, but I know it will pass - and later I will feel okay."

The conversation categories help focus our awareness on thoughts and talking. Affirmations help you do what you want to with thoughts or talking. Next we will look at structured experiences (exercises) which can be used to practice those control or intimacy skills the category systems have helped you identify and clarify.

Message Control by Affirmation

We send ourselves messages continuously, and many of those messages will influence us in ways we may not be aware of at the time. The principle of the affirmation is that our thoughts become messages to ourselves, and these messages produce consequences in our behavior which affects our lives. Positive statements about ourselves, our actions, thoughts, feelings, or attitudes are affirmations. Affirmations are one way we have of sending ourselves specific positive messages that will have positive effects on our lives.

An affirmation is designed to correct some aspect of negative thinking that has influenced us. Usually we don't recognize the negative messages. Rather, they are disguised as a point of view that is very often labeled as "being realistic." As you think about some of the following messages, be aware that even though they are negative we may believe that they "protect" us in our close relations, and in our everyday life.

We have sent ourselves messages by repeating negative thoughts about our limitations, our control, and our own skill:

"I can't do that well."

"That just seems to upset me."

"That kind of thing turns me off."

We have also sent ourselves messages about the world, about trusting others, about closeness with others and our control with others:

"You need to be careful about what you say to whom."

"People will push you around if you let them."

"I can only be close to a very few people."

These and other negative messages become part of us in our subconscious processes and our attitude patterns, and are reflected in the way we walk, talk and express ourselves nonverbally.

What does the affirmation do? *The affirmation is a tool used to mobilize your resources to focus on and achieve goals.* Think about the affirmation process carefully to clarify and understand your goals. Imagine, and try to visualize, the consequences of achieving your goals. Are you comfortable with these consequences? The affirmation may be used with greatest success if you understand its consequences:

Do you understand how it will change you?

How will it affect you?

Will you be satisfied with the affirmed goal?

Do you need it, whatever it is?

An affirmation has many qualities. An affirmation:

1. Uses positive words and a visual concept.

2. Is a statement that is made in the present.

3. Is a positive statement which may be an old negative statement reworded.

4. Is consistent with the *real* limits of the person and is focused on what a person can do - not what the person knows is impossible.

5. Is practiced by visualizing the goal condition stated in the affirmation.

There are a number of ways to *practice an affirmation:*

a. Close your eyes and imagine yourself acting in ways consistent with the affirmation.

b. Write the affirmation over and over. Give yourself an opportunity to respond to it each time you write it. Write the affirmation, then visualize it.

c. Repeat the affirmation into a tape recorder again and again. Leave time for a response. Always include an opportunity to visualize the target condition(s).

d. You can also practice the affirmation orally with another person. This may in fact be the best method, because the other person can provide feedback at various points in the process.

In order to see how this process works, we will describe an example. Remember that this example could be expressed or practiced in any of the ways described above. In this context, we will present it in written form. An example of a negative message I may send myself is:

I feel anxious when my wife criticizes me. This message may be rewarded as:

1. I feel OK with my wife's concern for me expressed as criticism.
2. I feel accepted and loved when my wife shows interest in me by criticizing me.
3. It's OK for me to feel anxious when my wife criticizes me.

There are a number of reworded forms which could be generated. For this example, we will trace a procedure that might be used with the first affirmation:

Affirmation	**Response**
1. I feel OK with my wife's concern for me expressed as criticism.	She's taking out her bad feelings on me.
2. I feel OK...criticism	It makes me angry.
3. I feel OK...criticism	I can't fool myself, it makes me feel bad.

4. I feel OK...criticism	I doubt my ability when criticized.
5. I feel OK...criticism	She probably feels bad.
6. I feel OK...criticism	It doesn't need to bother me.
7. I feel OK...criticism	She probably feels mad.
8. I feel OK...criticism	I feel OK.
9. I feel OK...criticism	If I remember she feels bad... in pain... I'll be OK.
10. I feel OK...criticism	Maybe I can help.

When you use this method, you will write your affirmation a total of ten times, and write ten responses to the affirmation. Write the affirmation once. Then, stop to think. When a response is clear, write it down, and write the affirmation again. Repeat this process until you have written the affirmation and your responses to it ten times.

This process is a specific example of a form of self hypnosis. You will be working to "deepen" your belief about something you do not yet wholly believe.

If you use the process you will be able to influence yourself in the desired direction. The affirmation works because *you* the user are effective.

The problem with affirmations is that *they only work as well as you do*. Like any other skill, the more you practice, the better you become at making them work for you.

Three Principles for Using Affirmations

Affirmations will work if they are used in a way that is *right for you*. The most significant principle for using them is *believe they will work* once you discover the best method for using them. To some extent, this "best method" is unique to you.

The second principle is *I can*. This internal message is repeated constantly to yourself during the affirmation process. No matter what the specific nature of the affirmation, the underlying message is that "I can help myself."

The third principle is *repetition*. We need to remind ourselves that "we can." Try out different procedures until you find one that feels right or until you know that you can use a variety of procedures.

Here are some steps you can take to practice the affirmation process:

1. Identify the feelings and expectations around the negative thought.

2. Decide what you want (the way you want to think).

3. Listen to yourself and others as you state your affirmation. You may want to use the written form we have suggested, or speak into a tape recorder. If you have the opportunity to work with another person, you gain an extra dimension of feedback.

4. Say your affirmation to yourself and to others as often as you can. Remember to do it whenever you need to feel better about yourself. You will be reversing the flow of negative messages to yourself.

5. Develop a shorthand procedure for the steps you use in the affirmation process:

a.*Identify* the area you want to change or modify.

b.*Monitor* your thoughts, feelings and conversation.

c.*Choose an affirmation* that feels comfortable.

d.*Repeat it* to yourself as often as you can.

e. *Say it publicly* as often as you can without feeling foolish.

Thinking Exercise

1. Write down your thoughts about your partner.

2. Classify them on the LOVIT and LOVCT scales.

3. Form an intimacy affirmation and a control affirmation about what you want your relationship with your partner to be in the near future. Each affirmation should be derived from the information that you gained in Step 2.

4. Repeat each affirmation ten times, while quietly sitting with your shoes off and your eyes closed. Breathe with a continuous flow of air through your lungs.

What is the Choice?

We need intimacy *and* control, in relation to both the self and others. The choice is clear. Do we want to invest our time and effort in trying out new feelings, attitudes and behaviors, or do we wish to simply follow the path we were on in the past?

The next chapter offers some exercises that can help us achieve desired changes in our behavior, attitudes and feelings. The exercises are focused on behavior change. The emphasis is on practicing behaviors that you may want to incorporate into your behavioral repertoire. The exercises are designed for groups of people. However, the first step involves thinking about behaviors, and considering the feelings and attitudes associated with those behaviors. This preparatory thinking is always an important step in the process of experimenting with or practicing new ways of behaving.

CHAPTER 5

Experiences with Intimacy and Control

Intimacy With Others

What do people need to better understand their relations with each other? How can we gain a clearer perspective on our relations with others and ourselves? And then, what can we do with our relationship insights and knowledge?

The focus of Chapters 2, 3 and 4 is on ways of examining intimacy and control in our relationships. Various procedures have been presented that allow the participant to examine her/his own attitudes and behaviors. Tools have been provided that the reader may use to gain feedback about his/her behavior and attitudes. But what will we do with the data from this feedback? The new understanding of the ways we are with others and ourselves may alone be enough to set in motion certain change processes.

Our plan is simple. We have made the assumption that people *can* change themselves so that they attain their relationship goals. Change will only happen if the person who desires different outcomes is the initiator of the change behavior. To be an initiator one needs tools to facilitate changes. Our models of intimacy and control are tools. The most significant part of the operational procedure is the "structured experience" or "exercise." There are four steps in the procedure:

1. Goal clarification. This is accomplished through examination of goals, expectations, and assumptions about intimacy and control.

2. Attitude Feedback. Two types of information are gathered in this part of the plan. First, we consider attitudes toward intimacy and control in relationships, second, perceptions of how the person says he/she will interact with others relative to intimacy and control. The instruments used in this process are found in Chapter2.

3. Behavior Feedback. Two systemic ways of observing one's behavior and analyzing it in the search for insight are presented in Chpaters 3 and 4.

4. Exploration of Attitude and Behaviors - This final step in our procedure may be the most important. It seems to occur naturally in almost everyone's life. We are all given feedback and, that leads us to think about ways to change or adjust ourselves.

It is our belief that learning effective verbal skills can remove the barriers to more satisfying relationships with one's self and others. It is particularly important to learn to use the three most intimate categories of verbal communication more easily and naturally:

> 8: Expression of attitudes, judgments, and indirect feelings toward others present,
>
> 9: Describing what is happening now to those persons present,
>
> 10: Direct expression of feeling toward those present.

These are the categories that seem to give most people the greatest difficulty. Skill and comfort with these categories of talk will do much to help people overcome their fears. Their skill will encourage them to take the risk to get involved, and surmount the communication barriers.

Level 8
Expressions of Attitude, Value Judgment and Indirect Feeling Toward People that Are Present.

Description: Complimentary remarks, praise, criticism, sarcasm, cutting wit, evaluations, apologies, rationalizing, denial, defensiveness, moral judgment, recommendations, instructions, advice, probing questions about other's feelings, and assumptions about the feelings of another person in the present group are all examples that characterize level eight.

Importance: People who are talking on this eighth level of intimacy seem to mask or control a wide variety of strong feelings with indirectness. Talk in this category is often stated rationally, but the tone of voice and body language may indicate intense feelings. The atmosphere of discussion in this category may be tense and uncomfortable.

At this level, people may be operating emotionally without clearly understanding the specific feelings. Feelings expressed indirectly may be positive or negative, but often an excessive use of statements at this level produces misunderstanding, defensiveness, suspicion, or feelings of manipulation. Still, the use of Category 8 talk is important to the development of most relationships. People communicate much of what they are feeling in this way to avoid risk of confrontation or rejection. At the most intense moments in our most intimate relationships, we often speak at this level of intimacy. At times when criticism, judgment and evaluation are expressed, it is difficult to simply "say it like it is" directly. In the most intimate of relationships, love and conflict are characterized by talk that is often evaluative and judgmental, so these feelings are expressed indirectly. What is important is the overall pattern and effect of feeling expressions in the relationship.

Generally speaking, Level 8 statements can be classified as either positive or negative, but one of the problems with the excessive use of "eights" is that the messages are sometimes ambiguous and confusing. As you observe your own (or others') verbal communication, it might be valuable to compare your positive and negative behaviors; actually take note of the relative frequencies of your negativeness and your positiveness. The following is an index of emotional conflict through indirect expressions:

$$\text{Index of Emotional Conflict} = \frac{\text{Positive Indirect Expressions}}{\text{Negative Indirect Expressions}}$$

If the number in the numerator is significantly larger than the number in the denominator, how does this affect your level of misunderstanding or conflict?

Category 8 also can be used to produce other indices of interaction.

$$\text{Index of Emotional Communication} = \frac{\text{Indirect Expressions (Cat. 8)}}{\text{Direct Expressions (Cat. 10)}}$$

This comparison shows how comfortably a person expresses feelings to others, and can lead to some awareness of his/her style of sharing feelings. The relationship between Category 8 and Category 10 statements may also indicate the extent to which a person is aware of and able to label his/her feelings. Sometimes the use of an 8 simply means the person is not aware of the feeling he/she is expressing.

In other words, Category 8 talk does not clearly include *owning* or *labeling* the feeling. The feeling is said to be expressed indirectly when the criteria of owning and labeling are not met. The most frequent indirect expressions of feelings are made through statements of value, opinion, questions and references, and statements that judge the other person, persons in the group, or things that have been said in the group. These are most often expressed as, "What you did/said was right or wrong, good or bad, appropriate or inappropriate." Other words that may signal the use of this category are *"ought* or *should"*. Some examples of judgmental statements are:

"This is a really terrific group."

"You shouldn't have done it that way."

"We really ought to try it, and I think it will be better than what we did."

"You made a mistake in the way you expressed that feeling."

"The way you handled that did a lot of good for the group."

"Try that again, get some feedback, and you will do a better job."

"You can't do that, it's not good for the group."

"Wait a minute, Dear, you shouldn't talk that way to Eddie."

"You and I shouldn't let ourselves get into situations like this."

"I can't stand it when you do that."

"Where on Earth are we going?"

"You're a knockout tonight!"

"Most people would be upset about what you're doing."

You probably noticed a quality of vagueness in the examples just cited. Judgmental statements usually lack some explanation of the speaker's feelings, and require that the recipient ask a clarifying question, such as:

"What was wrong about what I said?"

"Why do you feel that way?"

"What am I wearing that you like?"

"What's bothering you about what I just said?"

Defensive or apologetic statements may also fall into this category. At times such explanatory statements serve to expand the communication and clarify feelings that were unclear. Often though, the feelings are still unclear if the speaker is feeling defensive or wrong and is reacting in a "knee jerk" way to simply avoid conflict. Such statements express a need to explain or defend one's behavior; examples include:

"I didn't mean to say what I did."

"I couldn't help it."

"I did it because I felt it would help clarify and explain why I did it."

"I always seem to get in trouble when I do this."

"Anybody would react that way."

"What can I say? When the kids are home I go nuts."

Some communications indicate an indirect expression of feeling through *denial* of any emotion or feeling. The act of denial itself usually indicates that a person has some emotional reaction to being confronted about having the feelings. It is usually apparent through choice of words, emphasis, tone of voice or some other nonverbal behavior that the person is expressing a feeling. Examples of the words and phrases commonly used include:

"I don't care—I really don't have any feelings about that!"

"That did *not* make me the least bit angry!"

"It never bothers me when people criticize me."

"I don't know why you think it bothers me. I do *not* feel attacked!"

"I don't feel defensive—I don't even care what you think or say about me."

"*You're* the angry one, not me!"

"I don't care *what* happens to us."

"Do anything you want to me. I'm past feeling."

"I can tell you're trying to get on my good side, but it'll never work!"

Emotion is sometimes expressed indirectly through the use of *questions.* The questioner is often tring to get the other person to take the risk of expressing his/her feelings directly. For example:

"How do you feel about that?"

"How angry do you feel?"

"Come on now, don't you like me just a little?"

"All right now, spill it. You've got something on your mind, haven't you?"

"Are you upset about something?"

"Do you feel better now?"

Another method of expressing feelings and emotions indirectly is through reference to some unspecified, general other(s). The statement is indirect because the criterion of *ownership of the feeling* is not met. When a person expresses emotion in this way it is not clear that the speaker is actually experiencing the feeling. Some examples of these expressions are:

"People get really angry over that kind of behavior."

"We certainly seem to enjoy this topic of discussion."

"This discussion is depressing us."

"One feels tense when one sees the conflict."

"Anyone would feel bad if that happened."

"I think we are feeling very uncomfortable about this."

"Women all feel bad about that."

"The group is very satisfied."

EXERCISE: EXPERIENCES WITH CATEGORY 8

A. Situation to Imagine:

Two good friends of the opposite sex have had a bad shouting argument, and haven't seen each other for two days. They unexpectedly bump into one another at the supermarket and begin to converse superficially as they walk out to the parking lot. They stop at the first person's car, and that person begins to apologize for his/her attitude and behavior: "I'm sorry for ....."

Persons needed for exercise:

1. A leader (if possible) for the discussion.

2. Two people to continue the conversation.

3. Others (if possible) to listen and participate in the discussion.

Let the situation continue its natural course, with one person apologizing in an insistent manner.

Discussion:

First have a general sharing of how it felt to role play the persons or to observe them. Share thoughts about what happened. Then the discussion may be focused on a few questions:

1. When was it clear that feelings were being indirectly expressed? What was the effect on both participants?

2. Did the effect of indirect expression of feeling seem to vary, depending on whether the feeling was positive or negative?

3.What "rules" can be stated for the constructive use of Category 8 statements? (Use that does not block good communication or intimacy.)

B. Situation to Imagine:

The professor of education views a graduate level course (s)he teaches as well-structured and traditional. The students, on the other hand, view the course as aimless, loosely-organized and non-traditional. At the end of the semester (s)he announces to the class: "I haven't mentioned this before, but I think we should have a final exam." Some of the students become very excited, upset and angry.

Persons needed for the exercise:

1. A teacher.

2. An angry student to confront him/her and do most of the talking.

3. Other students (if possible) who hold varying opinions.

Let the situation begin with the teacher's announcement. Continue the discussion for 5 minutes. The person who takes the teacher's role will not make a definite decision.

Discussion:

Share how it felt to be the persons involved, or those who observed. Talk about what happened. After that, talk about these questions:

1. What feelings may have motivated the teacher's decision to give a final test?

2. In what ways, directly and indirectly, did the students show their feelings?

3. What was it about the teacher's announcement that caused the excitement and anger?

C. Situation to Imagine:

Four people are seated in a restaurant. The waitress takes their orders, and then serves drinks. Person A knocks over a glass of wine which spills on Person B. Person A apologies profusely, trying to wipe up the wine with his/her napkin. Person B says that it's all right, but shows by nonverbal actions that angry feelings are being denied. Then Person C knocks over a glass of water which spills on Person D. Person C says: "Oops!" and hands her/his napkin to D, who says okay, but shows nonverbal angry feelings.

Persons needed for the exercise:

1. Four central participants.

2. A "waitress" and others to observe the interaction.

Exercise:

When the situation has continued for about 5 minutes after the second spilling, stop for discussion.

Discussion:

Share observations and feelings, and then talk about these questions:

1. In this situation, what effect did apologizing seem to have?

2. Under what conditions would apologizing have helped the situation?

3. How can a person be polite and still not deny his/her negative feelings?

D. Situation to Imagine:

Think of situations in which you have been *praised, complimented, judged* or *evaluated highly* by another person or persons.

Persons needed for the exercise:

1. At least two people.

Each person relates one or two incidents, and then talks about what made these apparently positive experiences feel pleasant or unpleasant. Note and discuss any differences.

Level 9: Descriptive Discussion of Experience with the People Present.

Description: Observations, descriptions, clarifications, generalizations regarding the present group or relationships, restatements, summarizations; assessments of persons, behaviors, or group behavior; requests for a direction of activity or plan of action, projections regarding the present group's experience, requests for personal need fulfillment from others, and other statements that suggest immediate focus on the present group.

Importance: This 9th level of intimacy centers around descriptions and observations of the present group of two or more people. It contains statements about the group's status in the immediate present or related to past or future events as these affect the group now. Simply stated, this level provides feedback for a person or persons.

Feelings: There may be a variety of feelings experienced at this level of interaction. For example, one might feel challenged or caught, unfocused or confused, understood or devalued, elated or hostile, relieved or on the spot. At this level, the challenge is to see one's behavior systemically within the framework of a couple or a group. The purpose of Category 9 statements is to *create awareness of what is happening in the group at any given time.*

Descriptive discussion of present group experience

All the statements in Category 9 describe the "here and now" experience of the speaker. These types of verbal interaction can be divided into some specific behaviors. Here-and-now experiences are defined as events happening currently as well as anything which has occurred during the present meeting. This category is a very important one for couples or groups who want to *"understand what is happening to us."* It includes the following kinds of statements:

- *Expressions of feelings about self.*
- *Statements that attempt to clarify or restate another person's remark, for example: "I heard you say that the group is challenging authority."*
- *Statements that are group-oriented and deal with current nonverbal behaviors.*

Some examples of Category 9 are:

"It seems to me that you are very quiet today."

"I'm talking a lot more freely today."

"Every comment you made after that, you looked over to him."

"You just asked Jeff if he would give us some direction."

"The group doesn't seem to have a task right now, but what do we do when the group gets one and someone doesn't choose to go along?"

"People (referring to group) are very stiff about being observed."

"But I can see by your expression that it annoys you."

"I think that Charlie just made a suggestion we can handle."

"What did you do so long in the other room?"

"How does what you said relate to me?"

"Even when you are asked to join in, you hold back."

"I would like to say a couple of things about what happened today."

"What are you thinking?"

"It's unusual for me to be as quiet as I have been today in group."

"You've had your arms folded and have been staring off for half an hour."

"I need a smile and some attention."

"He wants some work to do."

"Why are you so uncomfortable with the silence?"

"Now, let's analyze it."

"A penny for your thoughts."

Exercise: Descriptive Activity

1. In a large group, form threesomes for this exercise. This exercise may also be done by a couple.

2. If using threesomes, designate members as A, B, and C.

3. A writes 5 to 7 descriptive adjectives and behaviors about B.

4. B writes 5 to 7 descriptive adjectives and behaviors about C.

5. C writes 5 to 7 descriptive adjectives and behaviors about A.

6. Each person incorporates his/her list of adjectives and behaviors into a few descriptive sentences.

7. A reads aloud to B; B reads aloud to C; C reads aloud to A, each in turn. Refrain from reacting or interrupting during this process.

8. Each person reports how it felt to give and receive the feedback.

In order to get some idea about how you reacted to giving and receiving descriptive information about yourself, the following questions are provided to guide your reflective process:

Data Collection:

Complete the following 12 statements (individually and in writing):

1. When I receive descriptions about myself, I feel...

2. When I receive descriptions about myself, I look for...

3. When I receive descriptions about myself, I am likely to act...

4. When I receive descriptions about myself, I think...

5. When I give descriptive information to others, I feel...

6. When I give descriptive information to others I look for...

7. When I give descriptive information to others, I am likely to act...

8. When I give descriptive information to others, I think...

9. When I give descriptive information to others, they seem to look for...

10. When I give descriptive information to others, they seem to feel...

11. When I give descriptive information to others, they seem to behave...

12. When I give descriptive information to others, they seem to think...

Sharing

Each partner or participant in the threesome reads her/his responses to the other(s). Share commonalities and differences among one another's responses.

This Level 9 communication is a type of conversation that is not often encountered in our relations with others. Although it would be helpful in most situations to step back and describe what has been occurring in a relationship from time to time, this is rarely done. It is particularly useful to gain perspective through feedback when people are in conflict with one another. *The purpose of statements within this category is to produce true description from the point of view of the speaker.* If the speaker is able to use language that is *received as descriptive,* and the listener and speaker share and clarify their own perceptions of what is happening, they may gain valuable insight and strengthen their relationship.

Descriptive statements are purely objective. Judgmental statements are biased by the perceptions of the speaker. If you try to clarify your thoughts and your talk into two discrete categories (descriptive or judgmental) you will find that all words and statements do not fit neatly into one category or the other. Rather, there is a scale or continuum which extends from descriptive to judgmental, with gradations between the two extremes. We could picture it as follows:

Descriptive **Neutral** **Judgmental**

1 **5** **9**

Try to rank the following adjectives on the scale from descriptive to judgmental. Use a scale of 1-9 in which a word ranked 1 is purely descriptive. A word you consider neutral, neither descriptive or judgmental, is ranked 5; purely judgmental words are ranked 9. Try to use the entire range from 1 through 9.

- ☐ dominating
- ☐ bullying
- ☐ talkative
- ☐ assertive
- ☐ repetitive
- ☐ deliberate
- ☐ responsive
- ☐ quiet
- ☐ encouraging
- ☐ specific
- ☐ reactive

- ☐ silent
- ☐ careful
- ☐ stubborn
- ☐ persistent

After you have ranked the list of adjectives, meet with a partner and discuss your rankings with each other. After you have talked about your rankings then try ranking the adjectives on a scale of how much you are bothered when they are used to characterize you. Use a scale like the following:

Now meet with your partner and discuss your reactions to the words.

Level 10: Direct Expression of Feeling Toward the Group, Group Member(s), or Another Person

Importance: Expressing feelings is something that everyone does. Some of us reserve the direct expression for our most intimate "special" relationships. "I know how he feels about me because he tells me" is a statement that reflects the important meaning of this the highest level of verbal intimacy.

There is no denying the importance of physical closeness. For verbal beings, words are also important because the combination of verbal and nonverbal communication links people together. Direct expression of thought and feeling enables a person to send the clearest possible message to another person. Both positive and negative messages help people feel closer to one another. "I feel closer to you when you express your feelings to me directly because then I know how I affect you." When we express our feelings directly to another person, it leaves little to assume or wonder about what is happening in the relationship. Communicating in Category 10 an important skill because it clarifies the feelings that exist between and within people. Remember that it is the feelings between people that bring them together or push them apart.

Feelings: People are generally insecure or even frightened about saying to someone, "I am angry with you" or "I am attracted to you." These two statements of feeling are more likely to be said indirectly:

"You did a rotten thing to me."

"You really behaved irresponsibly."

"You are an attractive person."

For many people, a learning strategy for practicing the direct expression of feelings is helpful in making this behavioral change. We must learn, as well, to tolerate the discomfort, anxiety, embarrassment, tension, fear, and even panic associated with telling a person face-to-face how you are feeling about her/him at the present moment in time.

Exercise: Category 10 Activities #1

Information: Think of your membership in your group (or couple) as you complete the following items. Write down your response to all five items.

1. In this group I feel warm and close when...

2. In this group I feel attracted to...

3. In this group I feel angry at...

4. In this group I feel frustrated with...

5. In this group I feel...

The next five items ask you to speculate or predict something about other members of your group (or your partner).

1. In the group the other members (my partner) feel(s) warm and close when...

2. In the group the other members feel attracted to...

3. In the group the other members feel angry at...

4. In the group the other members feel frustrated with...

5. In the group the other members feel...

Sharing

Now share your responses to the first five statements with the other people in your group (or partner). After each person has read her/his responses, then share reactions. Discuss any differences or similarities among perceptions.

Relaxation Activity

1. Close your eyes and think about feelings you have when you are with a person whom you love, and who accepts you for who you are.

2. As you sit with eyes closed, try to name the feelings you have.

3. Think of those feeling words.

4. Go back in time and think about happy experiences. What feelings did you have? Again, silently name the feeling words in your thoughts.

5. Now come back to the present, with eyes still closed, and name to yourself the feelings you have about your present group (or partner). Now try to directly express the feelings you have identified to each other. Take turns. Of course a person may choose to "pass" at any time.

Exercise: Category 10 Activities #2:

1.Read this exercise completely before starting. Participants will pair up (form groups of two):

A. Interview one another about how each feels toward the other. The interviewer may ask:

"What feelings do you have about me that are positive?" The interviewee answers: "I feel attracted to you (or whatever feeling he/she has)."

Other examples of responses include:

"I like you."

"I feel good about you."

"I feel comfortable with you."

"I feel positive about you."

B. The interviewer then asks, "What feelings do you feel that are negative?"

Examples of answers:

"I feel uncomfortable with you."

"I feel annoyed at you."

"I feel afraid of you."

C. The interviewer then asks, "Do you have any other feelings toward me?"

The interviewee answers:

"I feel ___________."

In each case, the answers should include a feeling word.

D. After the interviewer has asked all three questions and received the partner's response, the pair changes roles and repeats the interview and response process.

When you and your partner have repeated all the steps, talk together about the exercise for a few minutes. Be sure to share your feelings about the exercise.

Examples of feelings:

"I feel uncomfortable."

"I feel excited."

"I am comfortable."

Remember, the person who is doing the interviewing is the questioner and listener. He/she may not talk except to ask the questions and respond with encouragements such as:

"Okay."

"Yes."

"I understand."

"Uh- huh."

"Go on."

Expanding Our Concept of Control in Human Relations.

What does the word *control* bring to mind? One person exercising influence over another? Telling another person what to do? Criticism? Manipulation? These are some of the common associations.

The words may seem negative, but their meanings don't necessarily refer to bad or even inappropriate situations. There are times at home, at work, in school or in a military unit when these words and their associated actions may be appropriate.

Another form of control that is less well understood and practiced involves saying and doing things that give power to another person, or helps the group attain more control.

Examples of this kind of control include asking a question of another, communicating that the other's statement has been understood, and offering support, or some kind of statement that strengthens the other's self concept. These communications draw people out, invite them to contribute, encourage them, and call out the best in them. At the same time the speaker is expressing control.

It is this kind of action—*empowering* another person, a couple or group, while exercising your own control— that is less understood, more difficult to do, and possibly the most lacking in human interaction.

The three sections which follow explain and present exercises in the levels of greatest verbal empowerment—mutual verbal control statements. Of course, all levels of talk are important to the understanding of control in human relations. As we saw in our study of intimacy, these three most advanced levels of control are usually done least well by us when we communicate.

Level 8: Questions for Clarification

Description: Questions related to a specific thing that has just been said or done. The question is usually fairly brief, even if it is asked in response to a complicated point.

Importance: This category of conversation is important because it means that a connection has been made between at least two persons. Someone, at least, has been listening to another person and wants to know more about what has been said. The speaker is invited to amplify and explain his/her remarks, and has control of the conversation while he/she is talking and being listened to. Further attention is focused on the speaker, who gains status and power. At the same time, the questioner is influential in giving focus to the remarks and offering importance to another.

Feelings: Feelings aroused during this kind of talk may include puzzlement, curiosity, concern and interest on the part of the questioner. The one who answers may also have mixed feelings of power and importance, pleasure, and uncertainty, as well as uneasiness about being put on the spot.

Challenge: The challenge of this level of conversation is to introduce and maintain this kind of exploratory contact with one another without turning the situation into one of attack ("Explain yourself!") and/or defense ("I have no more to say!").

Definition of examples:

The point of each question is to clarify what the person has said or done:

"Would you give an example of what you just said?"

"What do you mean?"

"Then you agree with what was said?"

"Did you say to turn right or left?"

"Did I hear you tell him you felt angry, or sad?"

Exercise: Experiences with Category 8

A. This exercise is suitable for groups of 2 to 6 persons. The task is to talk for ten minutes, and to follow three rules:

1. Each person may speak for no longer than 15 seconds at one time.

2. If there are 3 or more persons in the group, everyone must say something within each 5 minute period.

3. After the first speaker has spoken, anyone else must ask the previous speaker a question for clarification of what was said before making a personal statement.

Processing the Experience: After the 10 minutes has passed, stop for discussion. Talk about how it felt to have to listen to someone and ask a question about what was said before you were allowed to speak. Talk about how it feels to have only 15 seconds to speak, and to have to clarify what you have said. If used informally, what effect would these 3 rules have on ordinary conversation?

B. This exercise is used with groups of 3 persons. Hold a round of conversations in which two people talk to one another while the third one observes. The rule of conversation is that before a person can speak (after the first speaker) he or she must ask a question for clarification of what has just been said.

At the end of a five-minute period, the observer will comment about what has been happening, directly and indirectly. Take turns being observer. At the end of fifteen minutes, talk about why it may be hard for some people to ask a good question for clarification.

Level 9: Acknowledging Contributions of Others

Description: Acknowledging statements are responsive to the contribution of others. They say: "I am listening to, understanding, and accepting your message." "I am not evaluating it." "What you said is okay with me, just the way it is." "Even if you're angry or have other bad feelings, it's acceptable to me."

Importance: Talk on this level is important because it confirms that the speakers are saying something worth paying attention to as it is, without judgment, argument or explanation. Confidence and personal power is encouraged in all persons involved.

Feelings: Persons who are acknowledged usually feel good, feel that they belong in a meaningful sense. They may feel relaxed, happy, important, and most of all, they may feel accepted.

Challenge: The challenge of this level of talk is for participants to allow a period of personal expression and acceptance to go on for a while. Extended interchanges of acknowledgement are rare in conversation. It needs to take its place with all the other kinds of exchange, especially the more active, judgmental and argumentative talk. It is a relaxing, healing communication.

Definition and examples: The central message of accepting or acknowledging statement is, "I hear what you're saying." The category includes statements that summarize, restate or simply refer to what has just been said.

"Yes, go on."

"I see what you mean."

"You're feeling good today."

"Thank you."

"You seem upset."

"Okay."

"That's something to think about."

Exercise: Level 9 Control

1.This exercise is done in groups of three. Two people argue about some topic over which they have a personal disagreement. The third person sits as observer/judge. The rule of the argument is that before either person can give his opinion or express her ideas, (s)he must first reflect, summarize or restate what the other has just finished saying.

In the discussion, whenever a person fails to acknowledge the other's contribution before giving his/her own, the observer stops the argument and tells the speaker to being again. After about five minutes of talk, participants stop and change roles. Three rounds will provide everyone with an opportunity to speak and to observe/judge.

When they have finished three rounds, participants discuss these four questions:

A. How does it feel to be one of the talkers?

B. How does it feel to observe and judge?

C. What is it like to be stopped by the observer?

D. What is the effect on the argument of having each opinion acknowledged before it is opposed?

2.This is an exercise you can do on your own at a party, social gathering, restaurant, or other public place where people talk. Listen to a nearby conversation. How often does one person "acknowledge" the remarks of another? Under what circumstances does it happen? How does it affect the conversation? Is the person who acknowledges special or unusual in any other way?

Make plans with someone close to you so that each of you will carry out this exercise separately. Try making these observations several times at different places. Then meet with the other person to share your feelings.

Level 10: Positive Reaction

Description: The statements in this category are focused on and responsive to what the speaker is saying, and encourage the speaker. Level 10 talk includes positive evaluation, praise, statements of support and expressions of positive feeling.

Importance: Level 10 statements represent the closest kind of conversational contact between people. One person focuses on another with positive responses that may include an open expression of feeling with a positive emotional tone. One person empowers another in the most natural, forceful way possible. All persons involved usually feel more energetic, organized and powerful.

Feelings: Feelings elicited by this kind of talk are strong, warm and enjoyable. It is a time of glow and good feeling. On the other hand, because many people are not used to this sort of talk, it may produce some tension and anxiety. The person who gives positive reactions may feel uncomfortable about being "too nice," overly optimistic, committing to someone, or "going too far." The recipient may be embarrassed by the praise, or feel suspicious that (s)he is being conned or manipulated.

Challenge: The challenge of Level 10 talk is to control your learned negative reactions, enter into this kind of talk and enjoy giving and receiving positive reactions without qualifying them or weakening them with humor or sarcasm. In the process, trust will be developed, and each person will feel stronger and more confident.

Definition and examples: The essence of Level 10 is the message that: "I like what you're saying ... I like you, and your ideas are good ... I'm supporting you to go on and develop your ideas the way you're doing ... I feel 'built up' and I want you to feel that way too."

"I like you so much."

"I'm really attracted to you."

"I really like what you did."

"What you're doing is important."

"Thanks a lot, I don't know how I could have done it without you."

"That makes me happy to hear."

"Very good, go on."

"I could listen to you all night."

"Well said."

"I agree."

"Terrific."

"The group did a great job."

Exercise: Level 10 Control

1. This exercise is designed for groups of two; in a larger group, form dyads and then bring the entire group together to process the experience.

For about 5 minutes, the pairs talk together about any subject they choose. The role of one partner is to praise the other whenever (s)he feels an inner impulse to do so (no matter how small the urge, express it). The role of the other person is to accept the compliment with a simple "Thank you." Then change roles for another 5 minutes of talk. When you have finished, talk to each other about how it felt to give and receive praise and compliments. Consider your reactions from the beginning to the end of the exercise.

Sometimes praise is divided into three types:

a. No standard is referred to.("That was a good job.")

b. A public standard exists for the praise referred to. ("That was a good job. You remembered to clean up after yourself.")

c. Some private or personal standard or reason is given for the praise.("I really did like the job you did.")

Did the kind of praise given make any difference in the course of the conversation and/or for the feelings aroused?

2. In a group of two or more, go out to an eating place. After your orders have been placed, listen to the conversations at nearby tables for about five minutes. Then share your observations and perceptions:

a. What percent of the conversation was "positive reaction?"

b. Who spoke these "tens?" To whom?"

c. What was the usual effect on the receiver of the remarks?

We have presented some ideas for practicing behaviors that, in our experience, are seldom used in everyday interaction. Perhaps they are taken for granted. We emphasize these intimacy and control behaviors because they have the power to improve communication when used with skill. The exercises may seem artificial, but as you try out the behaviors in everyday situations, you will find that these statements can increase positive relations with others. Remember that whenever you choose to alter your behavior, you will experience some discomfort during the "as if..." transitional period of behaving *as if* the new action or talk was already part of your *behavioral* repertoire.

The focus in this chapter has been on the categories of talk that are more intimate and those that provide the other person, relationship or the group with more control in conversation. These categories have been emphasized because in our daily lives they are so under-used.

CHAPTER 6

Nonverbal Messages of Intimacy and Control

Imagine eleven people seated in a circle. One of them, an immaculately groomed young man, sits stiffly, legs together, arms crossed, and says:

"I want to be close to this group. I feel very comfortable with everyone here."

The words carry a message, and his tone of voice seems to convey the same meaning, yet the rest of the group members feel uneasy about his commitment. They feel a contradiction in his message that puts them on guard. The words sound true but the visual message his body is sending bears a different meaning.

Our bodies send a constant stream of messages as we converse verbally with one another. These messages are more spontaneous and, under less conscious control than our verbal messages. The meanings of these nonverbal messages may seem subtle and imprecise, but their impact on our intended receivers may be stronger than the impact of our words. *Our nonverbal behaviors can serve to reinforce or contradict our verbal messages.* At times when our verbal messages are unclear, the nonverbal information we send may serve to bring the real message into focus.

A simple formula defines communication:

Message sent from you to another =

Verbal oral language + Nonverbal vocal & physical behavior

Often our communications contain some strong emotional components. Our spoken words usually represent our thoughts and follow the rules of logic. Our nonverbal behavior often represents our emotional message. Think about popular songs. The lyrics carry a message, and the melody and rhythm create the hard-to-define aspect we think of as "the mood."

The verbal part of our communication is the message we intend to send. The nonverbal part is the message we inadvertently present. When we are aware of the power of our verbal and nonverbal messages, we can deliberately control both aspects so that the total communication is consistent, as intended.

Here are some ways that messages may be modified, clarified or entirely changed by the accompanying nonverbal behavior. Imagine someone saying:

"I have a message for you that is very important and I'm going to tell it to you now."

If this is the verbal message, then it can be sent most effectively by making sure the nonverbal message supports its clarity. If the speaker is unaware, nonverbal behaviors can detract from the effectiveness of the intended communication.

1. The vocal accompaniment can be unemotional, flat or neutral - a monotone with no variation in pitch, rhythm or pace.

2. Vocal subverbal noises may not support the rest of the verbal message - sighing, yawning, halting "uhs."

3.Physical behaviors may also distract the listener from the message - clothing, facial expression, eye contact, body movements. Delivering an important verbal message without contradictory distractions can and must be a conscious performance. When a message is critically important, the delivery is likely to convey tension and concern. The expression of emotion through behaviors of tension and concern gives the listener a heightened message of importance that mere words can't convey. By maintaining emotional control, some persons are able to plan their nonverbal communication as well as they plan their verbal communication to send exactly what they want the listener to receive.

Now consider the message:

"I want you to check with me first before you make plans for us."

The statement could be a direction, a request, or a demand. The statement could even be a suggestion, in that it is capable of being restated as, "If you make plans that concern me, then let me know about them." The complete meaning as received by a listener will probably be determined by the nonverbal behavior that accompanies the speaking.

In other words, our total being communicates to and with others. Communication may be divided into three parts: *verbal behavior, vocal behavior,* and *physical appearance and behavior.*

In this chapter, we are most interested in the two nonverbal parts that contribute to the messages that we send, and what their implications are with regard to intimacy and control.

1. *Vocal behavior* includes volume, tone of voice, voice patterns, and also random vocalizing such as humming, whistling, singing, coughing, sighing, moaning, and grunting. Vocal behavior accompanies verbal behavior, and may intentionally or unintentionally contradict the verbal message, as in the case of a compliment expressed in a sarcastic tone of voice or with exaggerated mocking tones. From tone of voice and volume, emotional states are often inferred, such as secrecy, confidentiality and upset. Along with the "noises" of vocalizing, silence also

communicates, though its message is not always clear. Vocal sounds tend to clarify, obscure or reinforce the verbal message.

We all are aware that there are sounds which are not quite words, that can be used to communicate agreement, disagreement, surprise, fear and other messages. Some of these are "uh oh," "ah ah!", "mm hmm." Some of these "sound words" or "vocal words" are meaningful because they actually reinforce the verbal message, physical behavior or both.

It is well known that some men and women have an extraordinary effect when they speak to individuals or to large groups of people. This is probably so because their vocal behavior *powerfully* complements and reinforces their verbal message.

2. *Physical appearance* is often the only consciously planned component of nonverbal behavior. Both the casual and the sloppy look may be carefully prearranged to send a particular message. Much information is inferred from physical appearance, and receivers are often influenced by stereotypes (e.g. social class, economic level, degree of refinement, age, political stance, etc.). Dressing in uniforms and costumes are deliberate strategies to send a message or create an impression that will influence others.

3. *Physical behavior* includes facial expression, eye contact, reaching out to touch, body movement and actions related to "territory" or personal distance between persons.

Facial expression is complex, and may give away or be a deliberate disguise to hide personal feelings. Facial expression may provide the most visible clue to the actual meaning of the verbal message because the face is usually the center of visual focus. Smiling, sneering, frowning, eyebrows raised, and mouth agape are all facial expressions that can affect the message intended and/or received. Some of these facial expressions and their meanings have made their way into our idiomatic language, and cliches, such as "keeping a stiff upper lip" or "gritting your teeth," and "tongue in cheek."

Eye contact is in a class all its own, because it is so powerful, and has many possible meanings or interpretations such as "I want you," "Come over here," "Hello," "I'm ok, you're ok," and "You're stupid." Lack of eye contact also has meaning, such as shyness, fear, anger, insecurity, or unwillingness to acknowledge a person. Many cultures see the eyes as the "windows of the soul," and thus staring into another's eyes can usually assure the truth of communication.

Body movements are countless. They may range from foot tapping and hand gestures to actual contact like hugging and kissing. They include body posture and walking style. In fact, so many are constantly occurring that listing them would be a complicated and perhaps meaningless task.

Territory and personal space behaviors include actions that convey feelings people have about the space directly around their bodies, as well as about the area they occupy for work or some other daily activity. How physically close you get or allow another person to be, and what behaviors of others you can accept comfortably in your office or your home are examples. Distance behaviors may depend on gender, the quality or closeness of your relationship with that person, the reason for your meeting, the time of day, the presence of other people, and so on. Acceptable behavior of others who are physically near you or in your home depend on personal limits and expectations that you have developed over your lifetime related to your person and your property. Incidentally, within your home, your physical behavior and the arrangements of possessions send messages to others about your openness, formality and control.

One executive may have a neat, tidy desk and office combined with a formal attitude and communication style. His nonverbal communication tells his secretary and anyone else that lounging around in his office or taking the liberty of sitting on the edge of his desk would be absolutely forbidden.

Another executive may encourage and convey informality through his cluttered or informal office. He may physically touch his employees in a friendly or supportive way.

One person's automobile looks well-lived-in. He continually moves objects around to accommodate passenger seating.

Another person's car is immaculate and uncluttered. That driver sits rigidly behind the wheel. All persons who want rides in this car probably expect to adhere to strict rules: fasten seat belts, no smoking, no lowering of windows beyond a crack. The driver doesn't need to verbalize the rules; (s)he implies them nonverbally. In certain situations though, this person's children, or dog, may be permitted to break some of the sacred rules. It has been said that Sigmund Freud allowed patients to lie down on a couch not out of permissiveness or informality, but out of respect for their privacy needs when they spoke of sensitive, private things. We also know that people have favorite chairs, usual seats in restaurants, preferred seats in their offices, and so on. On a crowded elevator, people seem to defend the tiny spaces available to them by standing stiffly and avoiding eye contact, as if to protect themselves from attack.

Touch has potential to add emphasis and personal power to communication. Touching behavior may be conscious or unconscious, but either way it tends to strengthen or detract from the verbal message. The risk in touching may be that by violating the other's personal space, the entire message you intended to send may be lost. That person to whom you had been speaking cordially, though standing close to you, may *not* have wanted to be touched.

Perhaps as young children we enjoyed a wide variety of touching. As we grew up, we learned to erect barriers to protect ourselves from pain and to prevent unwelcome direct physical contact with other people.

Examples of Possible Messages Sent by Nonverbal Behavior in a Group (or Couple)

☐ Low intimacy, High control

- *Nods agreement without reference to the speaker.*
- *Reads books, newspapers, etc.*
- *Shakes fist at another person*
- *Frowns, expression of emotion*

☐ High Intimacy, High Control

- *Nods agreement toward the speaker.*
- *Puts arm around others.*
- *Shares food.*
- *Strokes other person's body.*
- *Moves toward group's center.*
- *Holds hands.*
- *Holds eye contact.*
- *Puts hand on shoulder.*
- *Smiles at other person.*
- *Hugs another person.*
- *Looks at several members in turn.*

☐ Low intimacy, Low Control

- *Stares at floor.*
- *Pushes body back in chair.*
- *Sucks on object (Pencil, etc.)*
- *Scratches part of body.*
- *Talks through hand, or inaudibly for other reason.*
- *Bites fingernails.*
- *Looks at watch.*
- *Doodles.*

- *Crochets, knits, etc.*
- *Twiddles thumbs.*
- *Looks at ceiling or wall when speaking.*

☐ High Intimacy, Low Control
- *Whispers to another*
- *Cries. Expression of emotion.*

The system we are using for nonverbal behavior is more general and not tied specifically to the verbal category system. What are some points of reference on a nonverbal intimacy scale?

Intimacy Nonverbal Behaviors

Low Intimacy Behaviors:

- *Eyes = little or no eye contact; glancing at eyes then darting away from person to other people not involved in interaction; looking down or off into space; totally looking away while talking to other person.*
- *Face-Head = rigid; no facial expression, no nodding or perhaps negative shaking of head; frown or knitted brow.*
- *Arms and Legs = crossing arms and / or legs; positioning so arms or legs interfere with or block message (example: put hand over mouth while talking or over face while talking or listening).*
- *Body-posture / position = body tightly held or turned away from other person; body tilted away from other person; actually moving away from other.*

High Intimacy Behaviors:

- *Eyes = continuous eye contact, mutual awareness of contact, steady and consistent, smiling, soft eyes, eyes focused on person while in conversation, pupils moderately large.*
- *Head-Face-Head = head nods in encouragement, acceptance or approval; face oriented toward other person, smile, relaxed features.*
- *Arms and Legs = arms / legs open, relaxed; no physical barriers in way of interaction.*
- *Body-posture-position = body unprotected; facing squarely toward other person; leaning toward other person, movement in direction of other person.*

Recent research on verbal intimacy suggests that the extreme ends of the intimacy scale are easily and consensually identified by people. Most people understand and act on the messages of nonverbal intimacy or distance which their culture promotes. Additional research on nonverbal behaviors suggests that the most extreme behaviors of the intimacy scale are clear to people but the more subtle acts may be confusing. For this reason, the Nonverbal Intimacy Behavior Scale does not define a continuum of categories, but rather presents behaviors at the extremes of low and high intimacy.

The nonverbal control scale is similar to the nonverbal intimacy scale in that it identifies behaviors at the extremes.

High Control Behaviors:

- *Silence - Confusion*
- *Eye Contact = eyes toward other; direct eye contact; unsmiling expression; serious, intense stare.*
- *Head-Face-Head = stern expression; frown; tight jaw;mouth tight lipped; shaking head "no."*
- *Arms / Legs = pointing, standing, rigid stance, folded arms, shaking finger, clenched fist.*
- *Body-Posture, Position = erect stiff rigid, forward movement.*

Low Control Behaviors:

- *Eye Contact = smiling; relaxed eye contact.*
- *Head-Face = soft facial expression; relaxed jaw; relaxed nodding.*
- *Arms / Legs = open; unprotecting; relaxed.*
- *Body-Posture-Position = open; relaxed; bent toward; forward movement.*

The following examples indicate how the nonverbal systems may be used:

At a small meeting, about thirty people are drinking coffee and conversing informally. A man (M) and woman (F) are making small talk.

Verbal	**Nonnverbal**
(M)Nice weather, huh.	(looking intensely, smiling, nodding)
(F)Silence.	(long eye contact, smile)
(M)You look good. Everything must be going well for you.	(moving closer open posture, smiling, eye contact)
(F)I feel OK, but things have not been going well.	(eye contact, serious intense focus toward other)
(M)I like you, I wish we had more chance to talk.	(moving closer, touching)
(F)Yeah, me too.	(cocks head in other's direction)
(M)Everyone here is so busy, the world is so complex.	(looking away, folding arms)
(F)Yes, so many demands on people.	(takes a step back)

(M)Well, see you after the meeting.	(Moving apart, seriousness in voice tone)

The issues raised by nonverbal behaviors have implications that are serious for relationships. They seem to fall into two conditions for our consideration:

1. The message is totally nonverbal. To some extent this appears to be a rare condition. People who share a relationship usually talk to one another, so it is somewhat unrealistic to think of nonverbal behaviors in isolation from verbal. However, there are situations that may be free of talking, and then the nonverbal messages by themselves are of prime importance. These situations may include eating, reading, watching TV or any other activity that can be conducted alone yet in the presence of others. Other examples include situations in which people have visual contact but do not talk because of distance or distraction.

2. Talking is going on and nonverbal messages are also being sent. This situation occurs most of the time. Even talking on the phone cannot eliminate the nonverbal messages since tone, volume and pacing of verbal messages are really nonverbal clues to the meaning of the message. Nonverbal communication behaviors are important because they often provide the essential emotional definition of the verbal message.

The nonverbal impact behind the verbal message may support, confuse, or invalidate the verbal message. An example can be used to clarify this principle.

A man, interested in a woman, says to her:

"I wish we could talk. I would like to get to know you better." (Because he is afraid she is not as interested as he is, his nonverbal behavior includes no eye contact, folded arms, and looking away.)

She says: "Really? You seem occupied elsewhere. What's going on?"

If you are aware that more than what you say is involved in the messages you send, then you will probably be able to adjust your nonverbal mannerisms to convey what you intend.

Some people work in occupations where they actually plan the way they will talk to others. Sales people are known to plan their presentations, even down to the nonverbal strategies. Supervisors plan their feedback sessions with workers. Doctors plan how they will tell a patient bad news. Probably you can add to this list, and become more aware that many others and rehearse their nonverbal behaviors.

Research through the years has indicated that nonverbal behaviors communicate a large part of most messages. Once we accept this reality, we must face the fact that our skill at decoding nonverbal messages are not nearly as developed as our ability to understand verbal messages.

Awareness of one's own nonverbal behavior, is a first step in gaining control of our communication so that our messages are received as we intended them.

How do I increase my awareness of my own nonverbal messages?

We can become more focused on ourselves in a systematic way. Use the following check list as a guide.

I 1. Am I looking at the speaker?
Yes __ No __

C 2. What is the expression on my face?
Positive ___Negative ___Neutral ___

I 3. Am I making eye contact in a substantial part of the interaction?
Yes ___No ___

C 4. Are my arms crossed?

Yes ___No ___

C 5. Do I nod encouragement as the person is talking?
Yes ___No ___

I 6. When speaking, do I look directly at the person(s) to whom I am talking?
Yes ___ No ___

C 7. Do I point my finger or use other hand gestures while talking to another person?
Yes ___No ___

I 8. Do I orient my body toward the person with whom I am talking?
Yes ___No ___

C 9. Do I put my hands on my face while interacting with another?
Yes ___No ___

I 10. Do I smile while listening to another person?
Yes ___No ___

Each of the checklist items has been coded: Intimacy items have an "I" preceding the item number and control items are coded "C". This checklist may be used to gather data about the nonverbal aspects of control and intimacy.

We can use a scheme like this to help become more aware of our own and other's nonverbal behavior. Talking with your partner and exchanging feedback can be helpful in experiencing the effect of each other's nonverbal behavior.

Results of another research study suggest that restrictions placed on a small group's verbal or nonverbal behavior inhibit the development of group harmony. This effect is frequently seen in traditional classroom settings.

Similarly, in situations where verbal expression is accepted and nonverbal behavior is restricted (for example, when children dine with adults in a formal setting), verbal expressiveness will be limited by uneasy nonverbal behavior. This supports what common sense would predict. When life situations require restricted verbal or nonverbal communication, social development is inhibited.

Now let us look at one way that verbal and nonverbal messages may be analyzed simultaneously. We have drawn on our two verbal instruments (LOVIT and LOVCT), the nonverbal behavior table presented earlier in this chapter, and some hypotheses drawn from observation and experience.

EXAMPLE 1

If someone says... "I feel very angry about what you just did."
(tone and volume slightly elevated).

And Does... Puts hand on your shoulder, leans closer.

Then you are likely to get the message:

About Intimacy	About Control
I want to be open and honest with you	I'm going to do something to you now.
I feel close to you	I'm making a forceful two-way connection with you about this...

Comment on the messages: The total messages are relatively clear and not entirely pleasant.

EXAMPLE 2

The setting: An upper middle class living room, casually yet carefully decorated and arranged.

If someone says... "My dear, of course I spent last summer in the mountains and..." (a long, rambling story about what the person did last summer, — median volume, repetitious tone patterns.)

And Does... Takes off shoes. Lots of small movement of the body. Brings food intermittently.

Then you are likely to get the message:

About Intimacy	About Control
I want to be fairly close close to you.	I want to have moderate control over you now, and more in the long run.
I want to be close to you, though I have mixed feelings about it.	I have no interest in direct control. I would like to influence your opinion of me. Maybe we can become strong friends. Maybe not.

Comment on the messages: This situation may be a confusing one to the listener. It could make you mildly anxious. You can't relax and enjoy yourself, but you are attracted in other ways. You don't really feel like staying or leaving. The confusion comes from hearing the mixture of messages. What messages are you likely to send back, verbally and nonverbally? What will be the overall result in your relations, in terms of closeness and control?

EXERCISES IN NONVERBAL BEHAVIOR

1. *Young Woman In Red Dress*

A young college sophomore was highly religious and conservative about her person, yet at dances she wore short, tight-fitting, flaming-red, low-cut dresses. The young men assumed that she was liberal with her affections. Invariably, when they tried to take liberties, she resisted and reacted with outrage. This would leave the young men feeling confused and sometimes angry.

Her roommate observed this pattern, but could not think of a way to approach the young woman about the discrepancy between the nonverbal messages sent by her attire and her intent to be attractive yet proper. The young men did know how to tell her what they felt either.

Discuss:

a. What are the messages the young woman is sending? Can you provide some possible explanations about how this discrepant behavior could have developed? What could be potential consequences if no one takes the initiative to inform her of the effect her clothing has on young men's beliefs about her?.

b. Who would be most logical person(s) to approach her about change?

c. What kind of changes would you suggest? How could you make these suggestions with sensitivity?

2. Looking At Our Own Behavior

One way to learn about the nonverbal behavior of others is to become more aware of our own behavior. Designate a time period (as short as one day to as long as one week) to observe and record your nonverbal behavior. Note examples of incongruity between verbal and nonverbal messages (times when the words you say don't match what you appear to mean). Notice specific ways you nonverbally express your thoughts (body posturing). Then, choose someone with whom you spend a good deal of time and record *his/her* nonverbal behaviors. What kinds of conclusions or new realizations have you reached?

3. What's My Message?

In a small group of people with whom you feel comfortable, take turns role playing a variety of nonverbal behaviors:

(a) emotions—hurt, rejection, joy, surprise, anxiety.

(b) body posture — defensive, sexually aggressive, humiliated, annoyed.

Guess what messages are being portrayed. How adept are you at perceiving the messages the actor is sending? What nonverbal behaviors make interpreting verbal messages difficult (e.g., holding hand over mouth, etc.)?

4. Uh-Er-Ah?

List about 5 subverbal vocalizations, such as, "uh uh," "aha!" "ummmm", etc. Then use them in a discussion with a partner. Notice how and when you use them. Ask your partner for feedback about the feelings you were communicating when you used a subverbal vocalization.

CHAPTER 7

Self-Intimacy and Self-Control

Putting Everything Together

"I have a lot of self control."

"I lost control and screamed."

"I couldn't control the shaking in my voice."

"I'm in control of my life."

"I want to be alone with myself for a while."

"I'm not happy with myself now."

"I feel like I have it all together today."

"I don't feel in touch with myself."

"Now I feel complete."

"I feel disconnected."

These statements illustrate how we may use the ideas of intimacy and control with reference to ourselves. Let's consider further how they are often used. "Self control," for example, is usually considered an admirable trait and in most situations a necessity. But suppose that I over-control or even suppress my actions for years because of social pressures and family responsibilities. At the same time my feelings are in disorder. I have suppressed them for so long that they are just about forgotten. Then one day, seemingly without warning, I explode in a rage or fall deeply into an isolating depression. Are these extreme actions admirable or necessary? Is it not more admirable and more necessary that feelings be recognized and accepted, so that appropriate actions may be taken as emotions are experienced? If I choose to live in the moment, my actions may not please those around me, but at least they will not result in extreme and problematic future upheavals. The point is that it is useful to think of self control as body-mind synergy rather than as one part of you taking over and making another part do something.

The concept of "self-intimacy" refers also to that synergy of various parts of our self, especially our thoughts and feelings. It is a matter of inner awareness.

In this chapter we will explore how self-intimacy and self-control are keys to our relations with other people. First let's think about how they relate to each other. Self-intimacy and self-control are related in that they both require *knowledge* of one's self. Knowing our thoughts, feelings and actions leads to wholeness and integration: being in touch with our selves. This knowledge helps us focus energy, be organized, make decisions and take action. Think of it in terms of a simple equation:

Intimacy with myself = Knowledge of myself + Control of myself

This self knowledge includes both feelings and perceptions I have about myself and the things I do. This knowledge map leads to *harmony* among my thinking, feeling and actions. Thus it is not surprising that self knowledge is so crucial to intimacy and control.

How do we gain access to this important knowledge? Well, most of it simply comes naturally to each of us. Our most important behavior to assure access is careful listening and attention to our thoughts, our talk, our feelings, and our actions. Keeping a diary or journal of our thoughts, feelings and reactions can help us be in touch with ourselves.

Paying attention to what others say to and about us is very important as well. Obtaining this self knowledge through the perceptions of others usually helps us feel more "whole" (intimate with ourselves) and "able" (in control of ourselves).

Consider the following conversation:

<table>
<tr><td>Knowing and
understanding
one's self</td><td>leads to</td><td>Intimacy,
closeness
with one's self
feeling good
about
one's self</td><td>leads to</td><td>Intimacy,
closeness
with
others</td></tr>
<tr><td></td><td></td><td>Control,
power
in one's being
able to do
things</td><td>leads to</td><td>Control
shared
with
others</td></tr>
</table>

"I envy you, Helen. You seem to understand yourself so well."

"What do you mean? Nobody really understands herself."

"That's *not* what I mean. You don't kid yourself as much as other people do. Like last week in the store when you argued with that clerk at the check-out counter. Afterward you just said you got upset and angry. You didn't say you were just joking or that it was a fight with some ignorant, silly person. You knew you got personally angry over a difference of opinion."

"Really?"

"Yeah. I think of you as a more balanced person because you're that way. In the long run, you *don't* get upset as much."

"When I do, it's a real one, though!"

"I know. But I still think it makes a difference because you *know* what you've done. I get a different feeling when I'm with you. Less tense, even when I know you're angry. I feel comfortable around you."

"I like being with you too. I always feel that I can stop by when I want to."

Some recent pilot research supports the idea that self-intimacy, intimacy with others, self-control, and control with others are all directly related. Positive attitudes toward self-intimacy, close relations with others, feeling in control of one's self and wanting to share control in relationships with others appear to cluster together. That is, if a person values one or more of these attributes, (s)he is likely to rank the others highly as well. This relationship among attitudes of intimacy and control appears to hold as well for people whose attitudes fall at the negative end of the scales, so that a person who has great resistance to close relationships with others, for example, is also likely to devalue being in touch with his/her inner self, experience a low level of self-control and want someone to be in control of his/her interpersonal relationships.

How does a positive relation between control and intimacy start? Think of it as starting *inside yourself*. You are aware of yourself, and have the tools and skills to increase your self-awareness. If you can accept yourself, you usually feel secure: in good control of yourself and emotionally receptive. Remember that "in good control" means having the freedom to choose from a self-determined range of behaviors. Emotional receptivity refers to a state of openness to experience feelings anywhere along an emotional range from anger to joy (rather than numbness or other unclear feeling). This inner condition can be thought of as heightened self-knowledge which is noticebly expressed in your talk and nonverbal behavior, much as other favorable inner conditions like happiness, confidence or good ideas readily show in your eyes.

Other people naturally respond favorably to you when you exhibit this condition. Even showing anger (rather than trying to hide it) can help create a favorable impression. Appropriate verbal and nonverbal expression of anger can reflect awareness, confidence and an acceptance of mutual control and direct expression of feeling. Others sense that they are being approached by an open, sensitive and accepting person. Being around a person who can effectively express a full range of emotions can help others safely move toward their own greater self knowledge.

Suppose you are *not* very aware or accepting of yourself. You are then likely to be insecure: victimized by circumstances, disorganized, and perhaps emotionally cold, numb, or anxious. Victimized or disorganized people are easily dictated to and rightfully feel out of control. Emotional coldness, numbness, or anxiety usually results when feelings have been suppressed, disregarded or disguised. This inner condition may be thought of as a lack of self knowldge and self acceptance.

This inner condition may appear as pretense, criticism, judgment/evaluation of others, negative reactions, and other indirect expressions of feelings. The insecure person may attempt to establish control through aggression or defensiveness. The other person(s) in the situation may tend to counter-attack in words or with gestures and other body expressions. Under these threatening conditions, low personal awareness and acceptance will limit the possibility for learning much more about one's self or the other(s).

We might say, overall, that awareness and acceptance of ourselves, and harmony of thought, feeling and action are essential ingredients in the development of high intimacy with others and mutual control. Experiencing high self intimacy and self control makes us naturally conscious of our connections with others. This consciousness leads the way to sensitivity with regard to others. It is convenient and practical for us to start with ourselves, and to assume responsibility for our own attitudes and behaviors. The focus here is on greater self awareness and acceptance—greater intellectual and emotional self knowledge leading to better relations with others!

What happens over time to a couple or group relationship? Typically there is a movement from issues and questions of *external control* ("Who will be in charge? How?") to those of *internal control* ("Now that we are closer, am I going to lose control of myself, or be taken advantage of?") In terms of intimacy, internal concerns typically emerge first ("How comfortable am I here? What are these feelings I have?"); over time concerns become increasingly external ("How close do I want to be with others? If I really give myself to this person or group, will I have to give up my individuality and my secrets too?").

Throughout this book, we have stressed the importance of talking in our relationships with others, especially talking with another person (or other persons) about one's own personal history of intimacy and control, and the feelings that accompanied those experiences. Connecting past experiences of interpersonal relations with those of the present has a positive effect on both our internal processes (who we are; where we want to stay and/or go with the people in our lives) and our here-and-now relationships with others.

We began this chapter by emphasizing *knowledge* as the key to intimacy and control. Knowledge is vital on personal, relational, professional and scientific levels.

How do we get this knowledge? What form does it take?

We have talked about the knowledge we gain through informal listening and observing. To help us get the *most* out of our listening, we have developed two instruments, the LOVIT and the LOVCT. These two instruments focus on talk, and allow us to know at any time where we and others are in terms of intimacy and control talk. This is reliable and useful knowledge.

Earlier in this chapter, the relationship between self control and self intimacy was briefly discussed. Research results have that shown a high positive relationship between self control and self intimacy, as reflected in responses to two scales: *The Self Intimacy Attitude Scale* [SIAS] and *The Self Control Attitude Scale* [SCAS]. We will now present these two scales completely, just as we presented the Intimacy Attitude Scale [IAS] and Control Attitude Scale {CAS} in Chapter 2.

Before we look at the SIAS and the SCAS, let's familiarize ourselves with the format used and some examples that will clarify these two scales. First of all, the SIAS and SCAS are constructed following the model used in the Intimacy Attitude Scale and the Control Attitude Scale.

Each scale has thirty-one (31) items. The SIAS contains 17 positive (+) items and 14 negative (-) items. The SCAS has 18 positive (+) items and 13 negative (-) items. The scoring procedure is the same as for the IAS and CAS (See Chapter 2).

The SIAS and SCAS use the same scoring system as the IAS and CAS. The positive score is computed by adding the ratings given to positive items, and ratings of the negative items are summed to yield a negative score. A "Total" score for each scale is derived by subtracting the negative score from the positive score.

Both the SIAS and SCAS have a positive and negative subscale. The positive subscale of the SIAS may be represented by statements like:

> "I'm feeling very positive about myself. I don't mind thinking about my personal concerns."
>
> "I get great satisfaction from looking within myself."
>
> "Being honest and open with yourself makes a person feel good all over."

Statements such as these reflect a positive orientation toward reactions to and knowledge about oneself. This self-positive point of view might be expressed as "I'm OK, I know myself, and am trying to get to know me even better."

The SIAS negative subscale is represented by the following statements:

> "Every person has an inner space that he/she doesn't try to examine."
>
> "People who seek greater self awareness are misguided."
>
> "I'm often my own worst critic."
>
> "I don't often think about how I really feel inside, because I'm afraid I won't understand myself."

These items suggest an orientation to knowing oneself that is resistant and lacks confidence. This point of view might be expressed by the statement: "I don't want to get to know myself because I may not like what I find."

The SCAS includes both the positive and negative attitudes that are within each of us. All of us, to some degree, are in conflict about how much knowledge we want about ourselves.

The positive scale for the Self Control Attitude Scale is illustrated by:

> "I can control myself, and if I want to let go I can."
>
> "I trust myself to do the appropriate thing."
>
> "If I want to do something I will do it."

One statement that might summarize the positive orientation toward self control is:

> "I trust myself, I feel in control and I can get what I want."

The negative scale is for the SCAS is illustrated by:

> "I am concerned about losing control of myself."
>
> "I tend to distrust myself."

> "I'm concerned about being carried away by my own thoughts and feelings."
>
> "I'm a rather impulsive person."

A statement that might summarize and in a sense represent the negative SCAS subscale could be:

> "I don't trust myself to be in control of myself and I fear sharing control with others."

These two scales, the SIAS and SCAS, are presented on the next several pages. You may use them much as you did the IAS and CAS in Chapter 2. Record your answers on a separate piece of paper rather than in the book.

After you have answered each item for the SIAS and SCAS, turn to the scoring instructions at the end of the instruments and determine your scores.

SELF INTIMACY ATTITUDE SCALE

The following items reflect feelings and attitudes that people have toward others and relationships with others. Specifically the items are concerned with attitudes of closeness, intimacy and trust. We would like you to respond in the following way:

> Please rate each of the following items on a scale of 1 through 9, where 1 represents strong DISAGREEMENT and 9 represents strong AGREEMENT. Do this by placing the appropriate number 1-9 in the blank space (on the left) of all items. Use the following scale as a guideline:

- 1. _____I don't often think about how I really feel inside because I'm afraid I won't understand myself.

- 2. _____I'm concerned sometimes about getting so involved in some personal project that I neglect other parts of my life.

- 3. _____I'm often my own worst critic.

+ 4. _____When I'm feeling very positive about myself, I don't mind thinking about my most personal concerns.

+ 5. _____I make it a practice to seek greater harmony in myself, and will examine my deepest feelings.

- 6. _____Thinking about my deepest feelings makes me aware of my inner conflicts.

+ 7. _____When I'm feeling happy about myself, I feel that there are strengths in me that are just beginning to come out.

+ 8. _____People get great satisfaction from looking within themselves reflectively.

+ 9. _____I spend a lot of time in seeking to know myself.

+ 10. _____I would like to get to the place where I could look within myself more easily and comfortably.

+ 11. _____I want to be able to focus on my own thoughts and feelings.

+ 12. _____I often want to examine my own feelings about another person.

- 13. _____Every person has a private inner space that even she/he doesn't try to examine.

- 14. _____I feel uneasy when I begin to think about intimacy and closeness.

- 15. _____I have concerns about getting lost in my own thoughts.

- 16. _____People must give up self control if they let a lot of their own deep feelings come to the surface.

+ 17. _____Being honest and open with yourself makes a person feel good all over.

+ 18. _____I accept all parts of myself and think of myself as interesting.

+ 19. _____Thinking about my sex life makes me feel content.

+ 20. _____Generally I feel as comfortable with the idea of a man friend as a woman friend.

- 21. _____It's easier for me to feel whole and sound in a place of natural beauty.

- 22. _____I want to be sure of my self control before I think about my deeper feelings.

- 23. _____Some of my own special commitments to myself prevent me from becoming a better human being.

+ 24. _____Being naked helps me to be in touch with myself.

- 25. _____I think that people who seek greater self awareness are misguided.

+ 26. _____When I know myself well, including all my feelings, I reduce the possibility of losing self control.

+ 27. _____Meditation is related to experiencing the physical sensations of one's body, but can exist without it.

- 28. _____Meditation and experiencing physical contact with oneself are the same and cannot exist separately.

+ 29. _____I can feel the most inner harmony when I enjoy regular physical activity.

- 30. _____My own tight schedule inhibits my ability to get in touch with myself.

+ 31. _____I understand and accept that I have among my deepest feelings some good feelings and bad feelings.

SELF CONTROL ATTITUDE SCALE

The following items reflect feelings and attitudes that people have toward others and relationships with others. Specifically, the items are concerned with attitudes of power, control and authority. We would like you to respond in the following way:

> Please rate each of the following items on a scale of 1 to 9, where 1 represents strong *disagreement* and 9 represents strong *agreement*. Do this by placing the appropriate number 1-9 before (on the left) each item. Use the following scale as a guideline:

- 1. ____There are a lot of things I just don't think about because of my own values.

- 2. ____I'm concerned about being "carried away" by my own thoughts and feelings.

- 3. ____I often drive myself.

\+ 4. ____I get really good ideas when I'm feeling in touch with myself.

\+ 5. ____I believe in equality of mind and body.

\- 6. ____I am a rather impulsive person.

\+ 7. ____On days when I feel in touch with myself, work comes a lot easier.

\+ 8. ____I am always the way I want to be.

\+ 9. ____I am neither over nor under confident.

\+ 10. ____I would like to be able to be the way I really want to be.

\+ 11. ____I can control myself and I can let go, if I want to.

\+ 12. ____I am often concerned about my own personal decision-making.

\- 13. ____There are some things about myself I don't trust.

\- 14. ____I tend to distrust myself.

\- 15. ____I am concerned about losing control over myself.

- 16. ____I take my work very seriously.

+ 17. ____I know if I want to do something I will do it.

+ 18. ____I don't think I'm a domineering person.

- 19. ____I am the dominant one in my sexual fantasies.

+ 20. ____I'm comfortable with both male and female aspects of life.

- 21. ____It's easier to feel in control of myself in pleasant surroundings.

- 22. ____I have to feel confident in a situation before I'll let myself go.

- 23. ____My commitment to myself prevents me from letting go.

+ 24. ____If I really want to do something I know I can do it.

- 25. ___The statement " know thyself" makes me feel uneasy.

+ 26. ____If I know myself well I will be unlikely to do something impulsive that I don't understand.

+ 27. ____I trust myself to do the appropriate thing.

+ 28. ____I am in control of my life.

+ 29. ____I like giving up control of myself.

+ 30. ____I am in control of myself but I can also let go.

+ 31. ____If I'm honest I know that sometimes I'll be tense and sometimes relaxed.

Our suggested procedure is as follows: Determine your positive, negative and total scores for the SIAS and SCAS. Follow the directions outlined on page 307.

1. Look at your *positive* score on the SIAS. Theoretically, scores can range from a low of 17 to a high of 153. Actual limits range from about 90 to 130. Check to see if your score is very low or very high. If the score is above 130, it could be considered high. A score below 80 would be low. The range between 90 and 130 may be considered typical, average or normal.

2. Look at specific items and see if there are any common themes in those items with which you expressed strong agreement (9) or strong disagreement (1).

3. Examine the *negative* scale in the same way as the positive scale. The theoretical range is 14 to 126, but the actual range is likely to be from 40 to 100. Certainly a score of 90 or above would be high and 40 or below would be low. Check to see if your score is very high or very low.

4. Again, check items you rated 1 or 9 for thematic similarities.

5. Now complete a *total* score by subtracting your negative score from your positive score. The theoretical range of the total score is determined by subtracting the highest possible negative score from the lowest possible positive score. The lowest possible negative score would be found by subtracting the lowest negative score, from the highest positive score. The theoretical range would then vary from -109 to + 139. Actual scores range from 20 to 100. Scores close to 0 would be considered low; a score below 0 is rare. At the other end of the scale, scores above 100 are high.

6. SCAS scores are determined in a similar procedure. The only difference is that for the SCAS, the positive scale has 18 items and the negative scale has 13, so SCAS positive, negative and total subscores are slightly different from SIAS scores.

The theoretical range for the SCAS positive scale is 18 to 162. Actual scores vary from 50 to 150. Scores above 130 are high, and those below 90 would be low.

7. After you have checked your positive score against the range, study your responses for common themes among those items you rated 1 or 9.

8. The theoretical range for the SCAS *negative* scale is 13 to 117. The range of actual scores varies from about 20 to 90. Scores over 90 are considered high, and those below 20 would be low.

9. Again, the pattern of item responses may provide additional insights.

10. Compute your SCAS *total* score by subtracting your negative score from your positive score. The range of actual scores varies from 20 to 100. Any score above 80 is considered high; scores below 20 would be low. (The theoretical range of SCAS total scores varies from -99 to +149.)

These instruments may have provided you with some new ideas about yourself. On the other hand, it's possible that the results will tend to confirm what you already know about yourself.

Remember, that these instruments, and items are yours to use, not use, study, or avoid. In other words, you are in control.

The following questions are offered as guideline for gaining additional insights from the experience and process:

1. What were your thoughts as you read the question(s)?

2. Which items puzzled you?

3. Which items did you feel were poor, foolish, ridiculous or unethical?

4. Which items did you like?

5. Which items did you dislike?

6. Which items made you feel good or made you say, "That's me, that's the way I feel."

7. Which items did you refuse to answer?

8. Which items did you laugh at?

9. Which items made you angry?

10. Which items did you need to read several times?

11. Which items caused you to stop and think, or perhaps hesitate before you responded?

Our hope is that no matter what you do with the items, instruments, exercises, or ideas in this book, you will examine your own reactions because that is the focus of this chapter. The rest of the book is about your relationships with others, but this chapter is about your relationship with yourself.

Think about the earlier parts of this book as interventions focused on your relationships with others.

	You	**Other(s)**
Chapters 1-6send	receive(s) messages	 messages
Chapter 7	send & receive internal messages	
Chapters 1-6receive	send(s) messages	 messages

This chapter uses the same model as in earlier chapters, but it is designed as an *intrapersonal* intervention. The focus is on your relationship with yourself. Our goals are to facilitate your self-knowledge and to suggest a framework for you to use in thinking about your attitudes and reactions.

These two aspects of self-knowledge (self-intimacy and self-control) are clearly linked together. In order to clarify this, ask yourself the following questions:

1. What do I need in order to control myself?

2. What do I need to do in order to get to know myself?

3. How can I feel greater satisfaction with myself?

4. When I do something I don't like, how can I correct the mistake?

5. Under what conditions can I have one without the other? (For example, good self control with poor self intimacy or vice versa.)

THE PEDESTAL THEORY ANALYSIS OF THE INTIMACY/ CONTROL RELATIONSHIP

Let us consider a final application of the intimacy categories that can help you play the intimacy and power game within your own head. The Pedestal Analysis is a matrix that examines each intimacy/control category against a self assessment in the context of comparison to another or others. The three options in the pedestal analysis are One-up, One-down and Even. The idea for this analysis emerged from three influences, the greatest of which is the basic format of Eric Berne's Transactional Analysis options or roles of Parent, Adult and Child. We may think of these options or roles as three categories of interaction which allow an individual in a couple or in a group to examine how (s)he mentally compares self to another or others as they communicate. Woody Allen's description of his relationship with his former wife provided another influence: "When I was married to the first Mrs. Allen I tended to place her under a pedestal." The third influence was provided by British humorist Stephen Potter who offered a variety of hilarious strategies for being consistently perceived as "one-up" on the competition in his *One-Upmanship* manual.

In the Pedestal Analysis, each Intimacy/Control category is related to a perception of self compared to others which sets the tone for the emerging verbal or nonverbal communication. It is less a way of planning strategies than a way of looking at past or recent communication events. The Pedestal Theory analysis gives the user insight into the effects of internal self perception on intimate or control communication.

Simply stated, inside your own head you are constantly aware of feelings of superiority, inferiority and equality. When you are communicating from any level other than equality, the communication is most likely indirect and non-intimate.

The charts on the following pages link the Intimacy/Control Pedestal matrix with likely communication behaviors. Examine the examples for yourself to determine the impact of your self/other comparisons on your communication with others.

PEDESTAL THEORY ANALYSIS OF INTIMACY & CONTROL THE PEDESTAL CATEGORIES			
Intimacy Category	**One-Up**	**One-Down**	**Face to Face/Even**
1. Nonverbal Attraction No conversation	Pity the poor slob. Superior. Other not as "good." Someone I can get. Not much risk in initiating.	Fantasy - "Pie in the sky." They're too good for me. I have no chance. Too much risk of rejection, Person/group reachable. I can risk initiation. I might be afraid, but I'm as good as (s)he is.	This person or group is reachable. I can risk initiation. I might be afraid, but I am as good as he/she is.
2. Small Talk	Pomposity - I'll impress themwith knowledge or experience *or* I really have nothing to waste on them.	I'm dull, don't know what to talk about; I'm uncomfortable;I'll act big or act nervous; or talk about the weather.	Common/mutual interests; searching for and finding topics of intellectual conversation.
3. People in General	People "should." My orientation is the only correct one.	I'm insecure or unsure about what I believe. I may be wrong.	Clear. I'm clear about my beliefs and I'm open to yours.
4. Individual Experience Outside the Relationship	Bragging - self aggrandizement or underplay and patronizing.	Reluctant to share faults & disappointments phony self aggrandizement to coverup.	Honest exchange of experiences and common agenda.
5. Coversation About Others Not Present	Judgmental statements & opinions as though one is superior.	Concern over feelings, opinions, judgments of others as thuough they may reject.	Matter of fact discussion of others as if they were present.
6. Shared Experience Past or Future	Sharing of future hopes as definite plans.	Subtle, indirect sharing of hopes, as if undeserving of achievement.	Honest mutual sharing of hopes and concerns.
7. Individual Experience Feeling/ Reaction	Magnanimous or grandiose sharing or description of feelings. Manipulative or feigned sensitivity.	Reluctant to share feelings or emotional reactions. Embarrassed. Timid. Ashamed	Honest sharing of emotion on both sides w/o fear of being taken advantage of.
8. Indirect Expression of Feeling	Shoulds & other judgments about other(s) present. How they should behave or be.	Insecure testing of how the other(s) might feel w/o stating one's own feelings.	Bantering, easy commentary on each other's behaviors, qualities & feelings about each other.
9. Description of Shared Experience	Judgment, blaming, attack, or parental approving.	Defensiveness, as victim or attack & quick withdrawal.	Feedback. Honest behavioral description w/o fear of aggression or rejection.
10. Direct Expression of Feeling	No risk patronizing or overwhelming attack. Blaming & controlling.	Defensiveness. Whining. Acting the part of the victom or insecure admirer.	Sharing of honest feelings with intimate and honest agenda.

PEDESTAL THEORY ANALYSIS OF INTIMACY & CONTROL THE PEDESTAL CATEGORIES			
Control Category	**One-Up**	**One-Down**	**Face to Face/Even**
1. No Conversation	Pity the poor slob. Superior. Other not as "good." Someone I can beat. Not much risk.	Fantasy-"Pie in the sky." He/She/ They're too good for me. I have no chance. Great risk of defeat.	This person or group is reachable. I can risk initiation.. I might be afraid, but I'm as good as he/she is.
2. Negative Reaction	Negative judgment. "That was a stupid thing to do!" "What kind of job is that?" Belittling statement toward other person.	Tentative negative judgment. "Well, I guess that was okay, umh...maybe not." Fear of retaliation.	"I got angry when you did that." Direct expression of negative feeling as a result of other's behavior.
3. Corrective Feedback	"That was no way to do it. Why didn't you do it this way?" Definite negative assessment / past oriented. Offensive position.	"Are you sure that's the way?" Tentative/ negative assessment/past oriented. Fear of retaliation. Defensive position.	"This was my expectation. That is what you did. Next time will you do what I asked?" Formative feedback-chance to improve the future.
4. Direction	"Do it my way without question." Authoritarian stance Aggressive.	"Well, what do you think of doing it this way?" Laissez faire stance. Passive.	"These are the results I would like to achieve. This is the way I would like you to work. Any suggestions?" Assertive.
5. Suggestion or Advice	"It's a shame that didn't work, but there is only one way it will. Do it my way." Condescending stance.	"Something went wrong...an accident I guess. Maybe this will work." Tentative, symapthetic stance.	"Here are a few alternatives. What do you think? I like this one." Definite empathetic stance.
6. Information, Facts or Opinion	"I'll tell you what the real facts are, now that you're in trouble." Lecturing / condescending.	"I think this way, but you may be right. I thought that might work." Tentative sharing of unsure information.	"I accept your orientation to the problem. This is mine. Let's work together." Equal value of information.
7. Questions for Information	"Where did you get your facts before you took that ludicrous action?" Negative judgment question.	"I don't mean to question you, but are you sure? Maybe it's okay." Tentative retreating question.	"What is the procedure you used in the activity?" Definite, clear request for information.
8. Questions for Clarification	"Did you really believe that ridiculous strategy would work?" Negative judgment question.	"Just for curiosity, what does that mean? Oh, never mind, forgive me." Insecure question. Fear of seeming stupid.	"What was the thinking behind your strategy, in light of the overall plan?" Definite clear request for clarification.
9. Acknowledging, Attending, Accepting	"Not bad...not bad at all. Interesting viewpoint." Tentative acceptance, grudging acknowledgement.	"Oh my! I never would have thought of that. How brilliant of you." Adoration, "apple-polishing."	"I understand what you did, and I appreciate both the effort and the results." Matter of fact acknowledgement.
10. Positive Reaction	"How clever of you. That is reasonably good thinking. Better that I expected of you." Condescending / "left-handed" compliment	"Oh my! Thank you so much. You really saved me." Adoration, "apple-polishing."	"I really like and appreciate what you have done for me and the group." Matter of fact appreciation.

Exercise: Intimacy and Control in My Life

Look at the following chart, and then at the list of sample words and phrases. Fill in as many words or phrases as you can in each of the conditions (alone, with others, when working with things).

When you have finished, study the words you've filled in. Then write a few sentences about what you think the words tell you about yourself. (What is the connection between what you are like alone, and with others, and working with things?)

Intimacy in my Life

	I can usually control my:	*I cannot usually control my:*
When alone:		
When with others:		
When working with things (environment)		

Here is a list of sample words or phrases you might use to complete the exercise. What others come to your mind?

- *anger*
- *apathy*
- *boredom*
- *competitiveness*
- *desire to do work*
- *desire to move around*
- *desire to hurt others*
- *desire for attention*
- *energy*
- *envy*
- *feelings of hurt*
- *joy*
- *sadness*
- *hostility*
- *jealousy*
- *desire for revenge*
- *restlessness*
- *sexual feelings*
- *temper*
- *tension*
- *tiredness*

A CONCLUDING MESSAGE FROM THE AUTHORS

A good concluding message for any book probably should try to wrap things up in a nice, tidy package. A theme presented here has been one of a continuous process, of flowing in and out of groups and relationships. Recall the guiding questions we posed at the beginning: "How close shall I get?" and "Who will be in control?"

The processes suggested here can provide some answers, and help formulate new questions and goals as well.

At a time when machines and technology occupy much of our attention, we ask ourselves if we can learn to walk the tightrope of intimacy and control wherever it may take us in our organizations, friendships and families. Our hope is that we can. The rewards may be great and unexpected. Can happiness be far beyond? Perhaps the journey itself is more important than the goal.

BIBLIOGRAPHY

Abbott, Franklin (1990). *Men and Intimacy: Personal Accounts Exploring the dilemmas of modern male.* Freedom, CA: Crossing Press.

Allen, G. and Martin, C. (1971). *Intimacy, Sensitivity, Sex, and The Art of Love.* Chicago: Cowles Book Company.

Amidon, E., Kumor, V., and Treadwell, T. (1983). "Measurement of Intimacy Attitudes: The Intimacy Attitude Scale Revised." *Journal of Personality Assessment,* **47**, 6.

Amidon, E., Flanders, N., and Casper, I. (1985). *The Role of the Teacher in the Classroom,* Paul Amidon and Associates, St. Paul.

Amidon, E., and Kavanaugh, R. (1979). "The Observation of Intimacy in Groups." *Personnel and Guidance Journal,* **57**(9), 464-468.

Apsche, J. A. (1985). *Intimate Verbal Behavior in a Small Group.* Unpublished doctoral dissertation, Temple University, Philadelphia, PA.

Arsht, B. (1982). *Further Validity of the Levels of Verbal Intimacy.* Unpublished doctoral dissertation, Temple University, Philadelphia, PA.

Avery, M. (1991). *A Multidimensional Statistical Approach Assessing Factors in Close Relationships as Evaluated by the Interpersonal Relationship Attitude Scale and The Intimacy Attitude Scale.* Unpublished doctoral dissertation, Temple University, Philadelphia, PA.

Bach, G. and Wyden, P. (1968). *The Intimate Enemy.* NY: Avon Books.

Beck, G. (1977). *Relationships Between Intimacy Training Methods and Observed Frequency of Group Intimacy Statements: A Descriptive Study.* Unpublished doctoral dissertation, Temple University, Philadelphia, PA.

Berne, E. (1964) *Games People Play.* NY: Grove Press.

Brigham, T. (1989). *Attitudes Towards Intimacy: The Human and the Divine.* Unpublished doctoral dissertation, Temple University, Philadelphia, PA.

Bronstein, S.J. (1988). *The Experience of Dyadic Friendship Between Women.* Unpublished doctoral dissertation, Temple University, Philadelphia, PA.

Carr, J. B. (1988). *Crisis in Intimacy.* Pacific Grove, CA: Brooks/Cole.

Chelune, G. J., Robinson, J. T., and Kommar, M. J. (1984). "A Cognitive Interaction Model of Intimate Relationships." In Valeran, J. D. (Ed.), *Communication, Intimacy and Close Relationships.* NY: Academic Press.

Christian, E. (1990). *A Survey of Trust and Intimacy Attitudes in Social Relationships.* Unpublished doctoral dissertation, Temple University, Philadelphia, PA.

Clinebell, H. and Clinebell, C. (1970). *The Intimate Marriage.* NY: Harper & Row.

Crider, W. (1981). *A Comparison of Verbal Intimacy and Verbal Control Levels of Males and Females.* Unpublished doctoral dissertation, Temple University, Philadelphia, PA.

Cullen, T.J. (1985). *Group Therapy with the Mentally Retarded: Effects of Control and Intimacy.* Unpublished doctoral dissertation, Temple University, Philadelphia, PA.

Dahms, A. M. (1972). *Emotional Intimacy.* Colorado: Pruett Publishing Company.

Derlega, V. J. (1984). *Communication, Intimacy, and Close Relationships.* Orlando, FL.: Academic Press.

Edgar, S. (1990). *Attitudes Toward Intimacy, Self Power and Interpersonal Relationships in Young people from Divorced Families as Compared to Young People from Non-divorced Families.* Unpublished doctoral dissertation, Temple University, Philadelphia, PA.

Fisher, M., and Stricker, G. (Ed.) (1982). *Intimacy.* NY: Plenum Press.

Freed-Fagan, E. (1984). *Factors Related to Control in Interpersonal Relationships: Locus of Control, Self Concept, Sexual Orientation and Stress.* Unpublished doctoral dissertation, Temple University, Philadelphia, PA.

Getzoff-Goldstone, A. (1985). *Intimate Nonverbal Behavior in a Small Group.* Unpublished doctoral dissertation, Temple University, PA.

Getzow, E. (1981). *The Relationship Between Intimacy and Continuance in Psychotherapy Sessions.* Unpublished doctoral dissertation, Temple University, Philadelphia, PA

Hendricks, G. and Hendricks, K. (1985). *Centering and the Art of Intimacy.* Englewood Cliffs, NJ: Prentice Hall.

Hullinger, P.M. (1990). *Psychological and Qualitative Dimensions of Friendship Among Women: An Examination of Intimacy, Sex-role, Loneliness, Control and the Friendship Experience..* Unpublished doctoral dissertation, Temple University, Philadelphia, PA.

Jourard, S. (1971). *Self-disclosure, An Experimental Analysis of the Transparent Self.* NY: Wiley-Interscience.

Kavanaugh, R. (1976). *The Issue of Authority and Its Relationships to Leadership and Power.* Unpublished doctoral dissertation, Temple University, Philadelphia, PA

Kelley, H. (1983). *Close Relationships.* NY: W. H. Freeman (et al).

Koslosowski-Gager, P. (1988) *Stresss and the Spouses of Dental Students.* Unpublished doctoral dissertation, Temple University, Philadelphia, PA.

Malone, T. P. (1982). *The Art of Intimacy.* NY: Prentice Hall Press.

Merves-Okin, L. (1986). *Analysis of Intimacy in Marital Dyads.* Unpublished doctoral dissertation, Temple University, Philadelphia, PA.

Perlman, D., and Duck, S. (1987). *Intimate relationships: Development, Dynamics, and Deterioration.* Newbury Park, CA: Sage.

Poplawski, P. (1988). *Psychological and Qualitative Dimensions of Friendship Among Men: An Examination of Intimacy, Sex-role, Loneliness, Control and the Friendship Experience.* . Unpublished doctoral dissertation, Temple University, Philadelphia, PA.

Potter, S. (1951). *One-upmanship.* NY: Holt, Rinehart, and Winston.

Rozecki, E. (1991). *Individual Interpersonal Dependency and Its Impact on Attitudes Toward Relational Intimacy and Relational Power and Control.* Unpublished doctoral dissertation, Temple University, Philadelphia, PA.

Rubenstein, C. and Shaver, P. (1982). *In Search of Intimacy*. NY: Delacorte Press.

Sandler, L. N. (1979). *Jungian Personality Type, Interpersonal Need, and Intimacy: An Empirical Study of Four Instruments*. Unpublished doctoral dissertation, Temple University, Philadelphia, PA.

Saner. S. (1985). *Sex-role Programming and Its Effect on Relationships*. Unpublished doctoral dissertation, Temple University, Philadelphia, PA.

Silverman, M. L. (1978). *The Effects of Three Kinds of Disclosure Activities on Intimacy in Small Groups*. Unpublished doctoral dissertation, Temple University, Philadelphia, PA.

Silverstein, H. (1981). *Group Therapist's Atitudes Toward Co-therapy and Intimacy*. Unpublished doctoral dissertation, Temple University, Philadelphia, PA.

Skolnick, A. and Skolnick, J. (1974). *Intimacy, Family and Society*. Boston: Little, Brown & Company.

Solomon, M. F. (1989). *Narcissism and Intimacy: Love and Marriage in an Age of Confusion*. NY: Norton.

Stepanovich, P. (1989). *An Expository Study into the Relationship Between Intimacy and Influence within Groups*. Unpublished doctoral dissertation, Temple University, Philadelphia, PA.

Sternberg, R. J. (1988). *The Triangle of Love: Intimacy, Passion, Commitment*. NY: Basic Books.

Strauss, J. (1983). *Power and Control in Interpersonal Relationships: An Empirical Study of the Control Attitude Scale*. Unpublished doctoral dissertation, Temple University, Philadelphia, PA.

Treadwell, T. (1981). *Intimacy Attitude Scale: Its Structure, Reliablility and Validity*. Unpublished doctoral dissertation, Temple University, Philadelphia, PA.

Turner, J. (1983). *The Efects of Racial Group Composition and Interactive Teaching Methods upon Racial Attitudes and Interpersonal Trust*. Unpublished doctoral dissertation, Temple University, Philadelphia, PA.

Widra, J. (1980). *Self-concept, Interpersonal Attraction and Intimacy: An Empirical Study of Their Interrelationship*. Unpublished doctoral dissertation, Temple University, Philadelphia, PA.

Youngblood, N. (1989). *The Relationship Between Job Satisfaction and Verbal Interaction Style in Professional Nurses*. Unpublished doctoral dissertation, Temple University, Philadelphia, PA.

About the Authors

Edmund J. Amidon is Professor of Psychoeducational Processes and Chairperson of the Department of Psychological Studies in Education at Temple University in Philadelphia, PA.

Marilyn G. Amidon is a Clinical Psychologist and Certified School Psychologist in private practice in Elkins Park, PA. She is also a Family Counseling Consultant at Women in Transition in Philadelphia, PA.

Jack A. Apsche is Coordinator of Applied Behavior Analysis at the the Devereux Institute in West Chester, PA. He is also the Founding Editor of *Behavior Therapy: An International Journal*.

Michael L. Silverman is a Management Consultant and Psychotherapist in private practice and Adjunct Professor of Psychoeducational Processes at Temple University in Philadelphia, PA.

Eugene H. Stivers is Professor Emeritus of Psychoeducational Processes at Temple University in Philadelphia, PA. He is also a Fulbright-Hays Professor and is listed in American Men of Science and the National Register of Educational Researchers.

Index

A

B

C

D

E

F

G

I

Q

R

S

T

V

W